STUDY TO BE STRONG

STUDY TO BE STRONG

*Systematic Theology
and Principles of Behaviour*

Robert Wyeth

Library of Congress Control Number:		2019903398
ISBN:	Hardcover	978-1-9845-8908-8
	Softcover	978-1-9845-8907-1
	eBook	978-1-9845-8906-4

The verses I have used was based in italics and can be taken from the Holy Bible from the New International Version (NIV), 1987 by Hodder & Stoughton Ltd.

Print information available on the last page.

Rev. date: 03/25/2019

To order additional copies of this book, contact:
Xlibris
800-056-3182
www.Xlibrispublishing.co.uk
Orders@Xlibrispublishing.co.uk
791889

Contents

Part 1 - Systematic Theology

Part 2 - We Don't Trust the Bible?

Part 3 - Principles Of Behaviour

PART 1

Systematic Theology

SUMMARY OF 'SYSTEMATIC THEOLOGY'

There is only one way of finding out what the Bible teaches regarding theology and that is by going to the book and finding out. It avoids all Christian teaching or tradition, by being Bible-based.

There's a number of Protestant churches all around, so the study of theology is doomed to failure, for there is more than one idea of how the books should be formatted. Even so, each author presents his view of how the church is organised, with man-made church tradition. And that is even more so, when the Bible was finished, with several Christian views on the organisation that enfolds us, even today. It will get worse as the end of times draws even closer.

The Bible is not a book selected on themes, and several contain conflicting views, for: though the authors tried hard, they didn't have the book you can read today, the Bible. Sometimes even well-read scholars will violently disagree, and if you have several books on theology, or go out to find them, you will be astounded at the difference one person makes to the other.

But Jesus said at the end of his life on earth, as he was going to die, painfully:

May they be brought to complete unity to let the world know that you sent me. John ch.17 v23

The denominations that we have today in the Protestant churches are wrong, seriously wrong. What Jesus meant was that all of his Christians are one and the same. If you can't have complete unity with systematic theology, you have failed to see what Jesus meant. He understood that his Father and he were one. Why shouldn't you read the Bible to see what God is saying?

Then make my joy complete by being like-minded, having the same love, being one in spirit and purpose. Philippians ch.2 v1

The apostle Paul is reminding his readers by loving each other, agreeing with each other and working together with one mind and purpose. Working together with one mind and purpose, it the same reason as Christ meant before his death. If you can't have systematic theology, then you have failed to do what the apostle meant, and I am very sorry for you.

My work is that - studying the Bible - and I have produced the text to show what the Father, the Holy Spirit and Jesus wants you to know.

I know that what I have done is to repeat several verses, but it will be necessary to cover all the sections covering the subject. I can understand if a section is missing or if a section is half finished. But I am only human, so study the Scriptures and add to it the words that are missing. But only do it because the Bible has the quotations that allow you to add the missing parts.

CHRISTIAN TRADITION

Church tradition is a real enemy and gets in the way of what God has been saying to us in the Bible. Over the centuries, church tradition means well and helps many people, but sooner or later, church tradition takes over from what God has intended for us to think and do.

I would advise you to study the Bible:
Matthew ch.15 v3
Mark ch.7 v5-8
Acts ch.4 v17-19
2 Thessalonians ch.3 v6

So what do you do about it? The idea is to read and study the Scriptures. If you do that, Christian church tradition will be less of a hindrance and you make sure that what the Bible says is correct and right.

The Word of God is powerful and mighty. It reaches further than man's church made tradition. It will be better to accept that, than church tradition. Like in Acts, where the rulers, elders and teachers of the law met together and Peter and John had to face them in the Sanhedrin. They said, "We will only accept what God wants us to study." Peter and John were not educated like some of them were, elders and teachers of the law.

Peter and John were fishermen.

See Matthew ch.4 v18-22

CHRISTIAN REVELATION
The Bible

The Bible as its own interpreter
- Timothy had been taught the Holy Scriptures from childhood.
- David himself, speaking under the inspiration of the Holy Spirit, and
- O Sovereign Lord, creator of heaven and earth, the sea, and everything in them.
- You spoke long ago by the Holy Spirit, and
- The Jews were entrusted with the whole revelation of God.

From infancy you have known the holy Scriptures, which are able to make you wise for salvation through faith in Jesus Christ. 2 Timothy ch.3 v15

I would advise you to study the Bible:
Mark ch.12 v36
Acts ch.4 v24-26
Romans ch.3 v2

CHRISTIAN REVELATION
Inspiration of the Bible

The inspiration is God breathed
- Jesus said, "Haven't you read the Scriptures."
- The Holy Spirit predicted this long ago.
- None of these prophets were moved by the Holy Spirit.
- You must realise that no prophecy or Scripture ever came from human initiative.
- All Scripture is God-breathed and they are spoke from God.
- The Bible is useful in teaching, rebuking, correcting and training in righteousness, and
- Was given it so that the man of God may be thoroughly equipped for every good work.

All Scripture is God-breathed and is useful for teaching, rebuking, correcting and training in righteousness, so that the man of God may be thoroughly equipped for every good work. 2 Timothy ch.3 v16-17

I would advise you to study the Bible:
Matthew ch.19 v4
Acts ch.1 v15-17
2 Peter ch.1 v20-21

CHRISTIAN REVELATION
The Supremacy of the Bible

Warning against neglect or misuse
- But don't just listen to God's word, you must do what it says.
- So if you ignore the least commandment and teach others to do the same, and
- You will be called the least in the Kingdom of Heaven.
- If you add anything to what is written here.
- God will add to that person the plagues described in this book.
- If anyone removes any of the words from the book of prophecy, and
- God will remove that person's share in the tree of life, and
- This will result in their destruction.

Do not merely listen to the word, and so deceive yourself. Do what it says.
James ch.1 v22

I would advise you to study the Bible:
Matthew ch.5 v19
2 Peter ch.3 v16
Revelation ch.22 v18-19

CHRISTIAN REVELATION
Fulfilment of Prophecy

The testimony of Jesus
- The virgin will conceive a child and she will give birth to a son.
- God has anointed Jesus to bring good news to the poor.
- Jesus said, "The blind will see, the lame will walk and the deaf will hear," and
- The Spirit of the Lord is upon me.

The Spirit of the Sovereign Lord is on me, because the Lord has anointed me to preach the good news to the poor. Isaiah ch.61 v1

I would advise you to study the Bible:
Isaiah ch.7 v14-15; ch.35 v4-6
Matthew ch.1 v22-24; ch.11 v5
Luke ch.4 v18-19

THE GODHEAD
The Being of God

The being of God
- The fools say in their hearts that there is no God.
- For he looks down from heaven to see if anyone is truly wise and who seeks God, and
- Without faith it is impossible to please God.
- The person who comes to him must believe that he exists, and
- He rewards anyone who sincerely seeks him.

The fool says in his heart, "There is no God." They are corrupt, and their ways are vile. Psalm ch.51 v1

I would advise you to study the Bible:
Psalm ch.53 v1-3
Hebrews ch.11 v6

God the creator
- Who has understood the mind of the Lord?
- What is seen on earth is not from anything that can be seen.
- Who has measured the waters or the heavens or weighed the mountains?
- Since the creation of the world, God's invisible qualities have been clearly seen.

God's invisible qualities - his eternal power and divine nature - have been clearly seen, being understood from what has been made, so that men are without any excuse. Romans ch.1 v20

I would advise you to study the Bible:
Isaiah ch.40 v12-14
Romans ch.1 v18-19
Hebrews ch.11 v3

The reasons we can believe God
- To whom can you compare God?
- Who is God's equal?

- People must fear and reverence God himself.
- He gives all men life and breath and everything else.
- To him all nations are as nothing the customs of the people are worthless.

Before him all the nations are as nothing; they are regarded by him as worthless and less than nothing.
Isaiah ch.40 v17

See Isaiah ch.40 v18-25

THE GODHEAD
The Nature of God

Natural attributes
- In the beginning, God created the heavens and the earth.
- He works out everything with the purpose of his will.
- He is before all things, and in him all things hold together.
- He is the king; he is eternal, immortal, the only God.

In the beginning God created the heavens and the earth. Genesis ch.1 v1

I would advise you to study the Bible:
Ephesians ch.1 v11
Colossians ch.1 v17
1 Timothy ch.1 v17

He is God that knows me
- You have examined my heart and know everything about me.
- You see me when I travel and when I rest at home, and
- You are familiar with all my ways.
- Your worshippers must worship in spirit and in truth.

O Lord, you have searched me and you know me. Psalm ch.139 v1

I would advise you to study the Bible:
Psalm ch.139 v2-6
John ch.4 v23

Moral attributes
- Only God is truly good.
- We are made right with God by placing our faith in Jesus Christ.
- God said, "We would be holy and blameless and pure," to all who believe.

"Why do you call me good?" Jesus answered. "No one is good - except God alone." Mark ch.10 v18

I would advise you to study the Bible:
Romans ch.3 v21-22
Hebrews ch.7 v26

THE GODHEAD
The Holy Trinity

The Holy Trinity
- In the beginning God created the heavens and the earth. (The word God, *Elohim* in Hebrew is plural).
- Jesus said, "Go and make disciples baptising them in the name of the Father, Son and Holy Spirit."
- We have seen Jesus glory, and he came from the Father, and
- The Word became human and made his home among us.
- The Spirit of the Lord and will testify all about Jesus.

In the beginning God created the heavens and the earth. Genesis ch.1 v1

I would advise you to study the Bible:
Genesis ch.1 v2
Matthew ch.28 v19
John ch.1 v14; ch.15 v26

THE GODHEAD
God the Creator

God made everything
- God gave life to everything.
- We were chosen according to the plan of God himself.
- God made the skies, heavens and all the stars.
- He made the earth and the seas and everything in them.
- God made man, male and female, and
- By his will, they were created and have their being.
- He is before all things and in him all things hold together: God gives life to everything.

For you created all things, and by your will they were created and have their being. Revelation ch.4 v11

I would advise you to study the Bible:
Nehemiah ch.9 v6
Mark ch.10 v6
Colossians ch.1 v16-17
Ephesians ch.1 v11

THE GODHEAD
Angels

God made everything good including the angels
- God saw all he had made and it was very good, and
- All the angels sang for joy and they came into being.

God saw all that he had made, and it was very good. Genesis ch.1 v31

I would advise you to study the Bible:
Job ch.38 v4-7
Psalm 148 v2-5

They are spiritual beings
- God sent his angels as flames of fire.
- They would be invisible, they do not marry and they can no longer die.
- They are far greater in power and strength than men.

Yet even angels, although they are stronger and more powerful. 2 Peter ch.2 v11

I would advise you to study the Bible:
Matthew ch.22 v30
Luke ch.20 v36
Colossians ch.1 v16
Hebrews ch.1 v7

The angels are amongst us
- The angels are empowered with wisdom.
- They protect the young ones on earth, and
- They do not know everything about the future.

My Lord has wisdom like that of an angel of God. 2 Samuel ch.14 v20

I would advise you to study the Bible:
Matthew ch.18 v10; ch.24 v36

The number of angels
- There are a lot of angels.
- Numbering thousands upon thousands.

Then I looked and heard the voices of many angels, numbering thousands upon thousands, and ten thousand times ten thousand. Revelation ch.5 v11

See Matthew ch.26 v53-54

THE GODHEAD
Good Angels

Archangels they are a higher form of angel
- Gabriel stands before God.
- Michael was there through war in heaven.

I would advise you to study the Bible:
Luke ch.1 v19
Revelation ch.12 v7-8

Cherubim were destined to reveal the power of God
- The cherubim guard God when he goes about.
- They guard the Ark of the Covenant.
- They guard the way to the tree of life.

The Lord reigns let the nations tremble; he sits enthroned between the cherubim. Psalm ch.99 v1

I would advise you to study the Bible:
Genesis ch.3 v24
Hebrews ch.9 v5

Seraphim or Seraphs stands as servants around the throne
- The seraphim have six wings, and
- They call out to each other.
- Their voices shook the temple to its foundations.

See Isaiah ch.6 v2-4

Angels
- The angels rejoice over one sinner who repents.
- They protect God's people wherever they go.
- They fight God's battles, and
- They keep these instructions in the church.

There is rejoicing in the presence of the angels of God over one sinner who repents. Luke ch.15 v10

I would advise you to study the Bible:
Genesis ch.19 v10
Psalm ch.91 v11-12
1 Timothy ch.5 v21

THE GODHEAD
God's Providence

God's providence
- The Almighty can do no wrong.
- If God were to take back his spirit and withdraw his breath, all life would cease.
- The Lord does what pleases him, in the heavens, the sea, the clouds, the rain and the wind, and
- They did what your power and will had decided beforehand should happen.
- God will not forget you!
- See, I have written your name on the palms of my hands.
- Even the most desolate parts of your abandoned land will soon be crowded with your people.
- They will neither hunger nor thirst, and
- The searing sun will not reach them anymore.

But they did what your power and will had decided beforehand should happen.
Acts ch.4 v28

I would advise you to study the Bible:
Job ch.34 v10-15
Psalm ch.135 v6-7
Isaiah ch.49 v8-12; ch.49 v14-16, v19-21

He assumes full responsibility
- God knows what we will eat, what we will drink, what we will wear.
- He has decided the length of our lives.
- These things dominate the thoughts of unbelievers.
- Seek the kingdom of God and live righteously, and
- He will give you everything you need.

Each day has enough trouble of its own. Matthew ch.6 v34

I would advise you to study the Bible:
Job ch.14 v2-5
Matthew ch.6 v31-33

MAN AND SIN
The Origin of Man

God made man and woman
- God said, "Let us make man in our image, in our likeness."
- He breathed into man's nostrils the breath of life.
- The man became a living person.
- Then the Lord God made a woman from the rib, and he brought her to the man.
- God said, "Be fruitful and multiply, fill the earth and govern it."

The Lord God formed man from the dust of the ground and breathed into his nostrils the breath of life, and man became a living being. Genesis ch.2 v7

I would advise you to study the Bible:
Genesis ch.1 v26-30; ch.2 v21-25

Man is body, soul and spirit
- My soul praises the Lord and my spirit rejoices in God my Saviour.
- Paul said, "May your whole spirit, soul and body."
- It cuts between soul and spirit, between joint and marrow.
- It exposes our innermost thoughts and desires.

May your whole spirit, soul and body be kept blameless at the coming of our Lord Jesus Christ. 1 Thessalonians ch.5 v23

I would advise you to study the Bible:
Luke ch.1 v46-47
Hebrews ch.4 v12

MAN AND SIN
Bad Angels

Before man fell, Satan sinned
- Now the serpent was the shrewdest of the wild animals.
- He said to the woman, "Did God really say?"
- The woman was convinced and she wanted the wisdom it would give her.
- So she took some of the fruit and ate it.
- Then she gave some to her husband and he ate from it too.

See Genesis ch.3 v1-7

Some angels refused to maintain their assignments
- God didn't spare the angels when they sinned.
- Where the angels who did not stay within the limits of authority.
- The angels left the place where they belonged, but
- God put them in gloomy pits and chained in darkness.

For if God did not spare even the angels who sinned, but sent them to hell. 2 Peter ch.2 v4

I would advise you to study the Bible:
Jude ch.1 v6

Satan - was given over to jealousy
- Satan, you were blameless in all you did from the day you were created.
- You were the model of perfection, full of wisdom and exquisite in beauty.
- God ordained and anointed you as the mighty angelic guardian.
- Satan said, "I will climb to the highest heavens and be like the Most High."
- Your heart was filled with pride because of all your beauty.
- Your wisdom was corrupted by your love of splendour.
- Your rich commerce led you to violence, and you sinned.
- All who knew you are appalled at your fate.
- You have come to a terrible end.

I would advise you to study the Bible:
Isaiah ch.14 v13-17
Ezekiel ch.28 v12-19

The actions of Satan
- Satan himself masquerades as an angel of the light and where Satan has his throne.
- He rose up against Israel and incited David to take a census of Israel.
- Job was a blameless and upright man so Satan afflicted him with painful sores.
- Satan was standing by the side of the high priest Joshua to accuse him.
- Jesus was led by the Spirit into the desert to be tempted by the devil.
- Satan will be released from his prison and to gather the nations for battle.
- He had deceived them and was thrown in to the lake of burning sulphur.

I know where you live - where Satan has his throne. Yet you remain true to my name. Revelation ch.2 v13

I would advise you to study the Bible:
1 Chronicles ch.21 v1
Job ch.1 v7-12
Zechariah ch.3 v1-2
Matthew ch.4 v1; ch.25 v41
2 Corinthians ch.11 v14-15
Revelation ch.20 v7-10

Fallen angels
- The bad angels want to carry out Satan's desire.
- He was a murderer from the beginning, not holding to the truth.
- Your enemy the devil prowls around like a roaring lion.
- For the accuser of our brothers, who accused them before our God, day and night.
- The devil has been sinning from the beginning, and
- Because the prince of this world will now stand condemned.

You belong to your father, the devil, and you want to carry out your father's desire. John ch.8 v44

I would advise you to study the Bible:
John ch.16.v11
1 Peter ch.5 v8-9
1 John ch.3 v8
Revelation ch.12 v10

MAN AND SIN
The Fall of Man and Original Sin

The origin of evil
- Everyone knows that God doesn't sin!
- They know the truth about God because he has made it obvious to them.
- Through everything God made, his eternal power and divine nature are revealed.
- So they have no excuse for not knowing God.
- Adam's sin brought death, so death spread to everyone, for everyone sinned.
- For God did not spare even the angels who sinned.

So listen to me, you men of understanding. Far be it from God to do evil, from the Almighty to do wrong. Job ch.34 v10

I would advise you to study the Bible:
Romans ch.1 v18-20; ch.5 v12
2 Peter ch.2 v4

The conception of the fall
- God knew that Eve would be like him, knowing both good and evil.
- So Eve took some of the fruit and ate it, she gave the fruit to Adam.
- I was born a sinner—yes, from the moment my mother conceived me.
- I am not really the one doing wrong; it is sin living in me that does it.
- All of us used to live that way, following the passionate desires and inclinations of our sinful nature.
- By our very nature we were subject to God's anger, just like everyone else.

Surely I have been a sinner from birth, sinful from the time my mother conceived me. Psalm ch.51 v5

I would advise you to study the Bible:
Genesis ch.3 v1-7
Romans ch.7 v18-20
Ephesians ch.2 v1-3

Original sin
- The Lord observed the extent of human wickedness on the earth.
- He saw that everything they thought or imagined was consistently and totally evil.
- How short is life.
- How full of trouble they are.
- All have turned away; all have become corrupt.

All have turned aside, they have together become corrupt; there is no-one who does good, not even one. Psalm ch.14 v3

I would advise you to study the Bible:
Genesis ch.6 v5-7
Job ch.14 v1

MAN AND SIN
The Nature and Extent of Sin

The nature of sin
- Have mercy on me, O God, because of your unfailing love.
- Because of your great compassion, blot out the stain of my sins.
- For I recognise my rebellion; it haunts me day and night.
- I have done what is evil in your sight.
- Your judgement against me is just.
- For I was born a sinner - yes, from birth.

See Psalm ch.51 v1-6

The extent of sin
- Can a mortal be innocent before God?
- Can anyone born of a woman be pure?
- Everyone on earth was corrupt, and
- You will never enter the kingdom of Heaven!

God saw how corrupt the world had become, for all the people on earth had corrupted their ways. Genesis ch.6 v12

I would advise you to study the Bible:
Job ch.25 v4
Matthew ch.5 v18-20

Sin and the individual
- For the wages of sin is death.
- I know that what I am doing is wrong; it is sin living in me that does it.
- I know that nothing good lives in me, that is, in my sinful nature.
- I don't want to do what is wrong, but I do it anyway.
- The sinful nature is always hostile to God.
- It never did obey God's laws, and it never will.

For the wages of sin is death. Romans ch.6 v23

See Romans ch.7 v14-20; ch.8 v7

MAN AND SIN
Guilt and Retribution

Guilt
- God shows his anger from heaven against all sinful, wicked people.
- They know the truth about God, because he has made it obvious to them.
- Everything God made, they can clearly see his invisible qualities, so
- They have no excuse for not knowing God.
- But they wouldn't worship him as God, or even give him thanks.
- As a result, their minds became dark and confused.
- Claiming to be wise, they instead became utter fools.

See Romans ch.1 v18-23

God cannot be the author of sin
- The Lord is just! He is my rock! There is no evil in him!
- God is never tempted to do wrong, and he never tempts anyone else.
- Jesus said, "God is light, and there is no darkness in him at all."
- God created people to be virtuous.
- But they have each turned to follow their own downward path.
- Isaiah said, "I am doomed, for I am a sinful man."

When tempted, no-one should say, "God is tempting me." God cannot be tempted by evil, not does he tempt anyone. James ch.1 v13

I would advise you to study the Bible:
Isaiah ch.6 v5
Psalm ch.92 v15
Ecclesiastes ch.7 v29
James ch.1 v14-15
1 John ch.1 v5-7

Conscience
- For merely listening to the law doesn't make us right with God.
- Even Gentiles show that they know his law when they instinctively obey it, even without having heard it.

- For their own conscience and thoughts either accuse them, or tell them they are doing right.
- For the covenant deals only with food and drink and various cleansing ceremonies, and
- That were in effect only until a better system could be established.
- Our actions will show that we belong to the truth.
- We will be confident when we stand before God.
- Even if we feel guilty, God is greater than our feelings, and he knows everything.

I would advise you to study the Bible:
Romans ch.2 v13-15
Hebrews ch.9 v9-10
1 John ch.3 v19-20

The justice of retribution
- Does the Almighty twist what is right?
- Should not the Judge of all the earth do what is right?
- We know that God, in his justice, will punish anyone who does such things.
- Don't you see how wonderfully kind, tolerant, and patient God is with you?
- God does not show favouritism, for
- He alone has the power to save or to destroy.

For God does not show favouritism. Romans ch.2 v11

I would advise you to study the Bible:
Genesis ch.18 v25
Job ch.8 v3-4
Romans ch.2 v1-4
James ch.4 v12

MAN AND SIN
God's Eternal Purpose and Human Freedom

For the Christian to do God's work
- We are God's masterpiece.
- We are created in Christ Jesus to do good works.
- Which God has prepared for us to do, for
- For God is working in you.

For it is God who works in you to will and to act according to his good purpose. Philippians ch.2 v13

See Ephesians ch.2 v10

The nature of the purpose
- The Holy Spirit will not come to you, unless Jesus departs from the world.
- When he comes he will convict the world of sin, righteousness and judgement.
- God chose them and he called them to come to him, and
- He decided in advance to adopt us into his own family.

I would advise you to study the Bible:
John ch.16 v7-11
Romans ch.8 v29-30
Ephesians ch.1 v4-5

Electing grace
- Should you be jealous because God is kind to others?
- Are we saying, then, that God was unfair?
- So it is God who decides to show mercy, and
- We can neither choose it nor work for it.

I would advise you to study the Bible:
Matthew ch.20 v14-15
Romans ch.9 v14-16

Election

- For he choose us in advance and makes everything work out according to his plan.
- We have received an inheritance from God because we are united with Christ.
- For God's will is for us to be made holy, once for all time.

In him we were always chosen, having being predestined according to the plan of him who works out everything in conformity with the purpose of his will. Ephesians ch.1 v11

See Hebrews ch.10 v10

PERSON AND WORK OF CHRIST
His Divinity

Jesus divinity
- Though Jesus was God.
- He took the humble position of a slave, and
- Was born as a human being.

Who being in the very nature God, did not consider equality with God as something to be grasped. Philippians ch.2 v6

See Philippians ch.2 v7-8

His Godhead
- For in Christ lives all the fullness of God in a human body.
- He existed in the beginning with God.
- God created everything through him.
- The Word gave life to everything that was created.
- Even the wind and raging waves obey him.
- He even healed them all, demon-possessed, epileptic or paralysed.
- The Jews were going to stone him because he made himself equal with God.

For in Christ lives all the fullness of the Deity lives in bodily form. Colossians ch.2 v9

I would advise you to study the Bible:
Matthew ch.4 v23-25
Luke 8 v22-25
John ch.1 v1-5; ch.10 v29-33

PERSON AND WORK OF CHRIST
His Sonship

Jesus sonship
- Peter said, "You are the Messiah, the Son of the living God."
- The Father said, "You are my dearly loved Son, and you bring me great joy."
- The Son radiates God's own glory and expresses the very character of God.

The Son is the radiance of God's glory and the exact representation of his being, sustaining all things by his powerful word. Hebrews ch.1 v3

I would advise you to study the Bible:
Matthew ch.16 v16-17
Mark ch.1 v11

Son of the living God
- Jesus is the only true God.
- Christ is the visible image of the invisible God.
- Everything was created through him and for him and he holds creation together.
- God has given him authority over everyone, and
- Jesus gives eternal life to each one the Father has given to him.

His Son Jesus Christ. He is the true God and eternal life. 1 John ch.5 v20

I would advise you to study the Bible:
John ch.17 v1-5
Colossians ch.1 v15-17

PERSON AND WORK OF CHRIST
The Incarnation

Jesus incarnation
- God sent his Son when the time was right.
- He was born of a woman from the power of the Holy Spirit.
- He will be called: Wonderful Counsellor, Mighty God, Everlasting Father, Prince of Peace.
- Though he was God, he did not think of equality with God as something to cling to.
- The Spirit of the Lord will rest on Jesus.

But he had no union with her until she gave birth to a son. He gave him the name Jesus. Matthew ch.1 v25

I would advise you to study the Bible:
Isaiah ch.9 v6-7; ch.11 v1-3
Matthew ch.1 v18
Galatians ch.4 v4
Philippians ch.2 v6

Jesus was sinless
- Jesus had done no wrong and had never deceived anyone.
- He came to take away our sins, and there is no sin in him, and
- He sustains everything by the mighty power of his command.

And in him is no sin. 1 John ch.3 v5

I would advise you to study the Bible:
Isaiah ch.53 v9
Hebrews ch.1 v3-4; ch.4 v15

PERSON AND WORK OF CHRIST
Humanity

Jesus as a servant
- He gave up his divine privileges.
- He took the humble position of a slave and was born as a human being.
- In obedience to God and died a criminal's death on a cross.
- For there is only one God and one Mediator who can reconcile God and humanity.

For there is one God and one mediator between God and men, the man Christ Jesus. 1 Timothy ch.2 v5

See Philippians ch.2 v7-11

As God he was thinking and acted as a man
- But soon a fierce storm came down on the lake, when they were going across.
- The boat was filling with water, and they were in real danger.
- In his earthly life, he was born into King David's family line, and he died.
- On the cross, Jesus said, "My God, my God, why have you abandoned me?"
- For reconciling the world to himself.
- No longer counting people's sins against them.

God was reconciling the world to himself in Christ, not counting men's sins against them. 2 Corinthians ch.5 v19

I would advise you to study the Bible:
Matthew ch.27 v46
Luke ch.8 v22-23
Romans ch.1 v3-4

PERSON AND WORK OF CHRIST
The Life of Christ

Jesus life
- We have seen his glory, the glory of the Father's one and only Son.
- He has revealed God to us.
- He faced all of the same testings we do, yet he did not sin.
- Jesus grew in wisdom and in stature and in favour with God and all the people.
- He was full of unfailing love and faithfulness.
- If he died, then Jesus will send the Holy Spirit to you.

Jesus grew in wisdom and in stature, and in favour with God and men. Luke ch.2 v52

I would advise you to study the Bible:
Matthew ch.1 v21
Mark ch.4 v37-41
John ch.1 v14; ch.1 v18; ch.16 v7
Hebrews ch.4 v15

What he was known to have done
- His miracles

See Matthew ch.14 v22-33

- His teaching

See Matthew ch.13 v1-9

- His healing

See Matthew ch.17 v14-18

PERSON AND WORK OF CHRIST
The Death of Christ

Jesus death
- He suffered physical death, but he was raised to life in the Spirit.
- I know that the Lord is always with me.
- I will not be shaken, for he is right beside me.
- For you will not leave my soul among the dead or allow your holy one to rot in the grave.
- That is why Christ also descended to our lowly world.
- That is why the Good News was preached to those who are now dead.
- They will have to face God, who will judge everyone, both the living and the dead.
- He died for sinners to bring you safely home to God.

For Christ died for sins once for all, the righteous for the unrighteous, to bring you to God. 1 Peter ch.3 v18

I would advise you to study the Bible:
Psalm ch.16 v8-10
Ephesians ch.4 v9-10
1 Peter ch.3 v19-20; ch.4 v4-6

He will make the journey for us to follow
- But take heart, because Jesus has overcome the world.
- The bodies of many godly men and women who had died were raised from the dead, and
- Every tongue will confess that Jesus Christ is Lord, for
- I heard every creature in heaven and on earth praising the Lamb.

In this world you will have trouble. But take heart! I have overcome the world. John ch.16 v33

I would advise you to study the Bible:
Matthew ch.27 v52-53
Philippians ch.2 v10-11
Revelation ch.5 v13

PERSON AND WORK OF CHRIST
The Resurrection and Exaltation of Christ

The resurrection of Jesus
- Jesus appeared to his disciples after he was raised from the dead.
- After his suffering, he showed himself and gave many convincing proofs that he was alive.
- God exalted him to the highest place and he gave him a name that is above every name.
- At the name of Jesus every knee should bow in heaven and on earth.

This was now the third time Jesus appeared to his disciples after he was raised from the dead. John ch.21 v14

I would advise you to study the Bible:
John ch.11 v25-26
Acts ch.1 v3
Philippians ch.2 v9-11

The significance of the resurrection
- Christ Jesus has destroyed death and he has brought life and immortality.
- He is the living One, and he is alive forever and ever, and
- He holds the keys of death and the grave.

I am the Living One; I was dead, and behold I am alive for ever and ever! I hold the keys of death and Hades. Revelation ch.1 v18

See 2 Timothy ch.1 v10

The evidence for the fact of the resurrection
- Some of the guards went in to the city and reported what had happened.
- The chief priests and elders gave the soldiers a large sum of money.
- The disciples were together with the doors locked for fear of the Jews.
- But later the Holy Spirit appeared.
- The apostles were going out teaching the people, and
- They were proclaiming that Jesus was raised from the dead.
- The Lord added daily those who were being saved.

They were greatly disturbed because the apostles were teaching the people and proclaiming in Jesus the resurrection of the dead. Acts ch.4 v2

I would advise you to study the Bible:
Matthew ch.28 v11-15
John ch.20 v19-20
Acts ch.2 v41-47; ch.4 v1

The resurrection body of our Lord
- Mary said, "They have taken my Lord away and I don't know where to find him."
- The disciples' eyes were opened and they recognised him.
- They were startled and frightened thinking they saw a ghost.
- Jesus said, "Touch me and see."
- Jesus said, "A ghost does not have flesh and blood as you see I have look at my hands and feet, it is I myself," and
- He disappeared from their sight.

Look at my hands and feet. It is I myself! Touch me and see; a ghost does not have flesh and bones, as you see I have. Luke ch.24 v39

I would advise you to study the Bible:
Luke ch.24 v31; ch.24 v37-43
John ch.20 v13-15

The ascension of Jesus
- Jesus answered, "I was sent only to the lost sheep of Israel," for
- All authority in heaven and on earth has been given to me.
- "Therefore go and make disciples of all nations," said Jesus.
- Teach these new disciples to obey all the commands I have given you.
- The disciples began speaking as the Holy Spirit enabled them.

I was sent only to the lost sheep of Israel. Matthew ch.15 v24

I would advise you to study the Bible:
Matthew ch.28 v18-20
Acts ch.2 v1-4

PERSON AND WORK OF CHRIST
The Threefold Work of Christ

As a prophet
- The crowds answered, "This is Jesus the prophet."
- Jesus healed every kind of disease and illness, and
- He continues as prophet until the final restoration of all things.

And the crowds answered, "This is Jesus, the prophet from Nazareth in Galilee." Matthew ch.21 v11

I would advise you to study the Bible:
Matthew ch.4 v23-25
Acts ch.3 v21-22

As a priest
- Jesus set his face to go to Jerusalem, voluntarily laying down his life.
- He is able to save those who come to him.
- Because he always lives to intercede for them.
- For there is one mediator between God and men.

For there is one God and one mediator between God and men, the man Christ Jesus. 1 Timothy ch.2 v5

I would advise you to study the Bible:
Mark ch.8 v31
Luke ch.9 v51
Hebrews ch.7 v25

As a king
- Every tongue confess that Jesus Christ is Lord.
- God crowned him with glory and honour, and
- Gave him authority over all things.
- He will rule with fairness and justice for all eternity.

And every tongue confess that Jesus Christ is Lord. Philippians ch.2 v11

I would advise you to study the Bible:
Isaiah ch.9 v6-7
Hebrews ch.2 v5-8

DOCTRINE OF THE ATONEMENT
Theology of the Atonement

Old Testament illustration
- The Passover is the shedding of the blood of a lamb, but
- Jesus however will make it possible for our sins to be forgiven.

Because he poured out his life unto death. Isaiah ch.49 v12

I would advise you to study the Bible:
Exodus ch.12 v11-13
Isaiah ch.53 v10-12

Theology of the atonement
- Day after day every Israelite priest stands and performs his religious duties.
- This can never take away our sins.
- God had presented Jesus as a sacrifice for sin.
- It caused him to suffer and die.
- He did this to demonstrate his righteousness, for he himself is fair and just.
- God declares sinners to be right in his sight when they believe in Jesus.

For God presented him as a sacrifice for atonement. Romans ch.3 v25

I would advise you to study the Bible:
Romans ch.3 v26
Galatians ch.4 v4-5
Hebrews ch.10 v11-14

Equivalent of punishment
- "I take no pleasure in the death of wicked people," said God.
- For he loved the world so much that he gave his one and only Son.
- So that everyone who believes in Jesus will have eternal life.
- God sent his Son not to judge the world, but to save the world through him.
- Jesus laid down his life for all the sins of the whole world.

I am the good shepherd. The good shepherd lays down his life for the sheep.
John ch.10 v11

I would advise you to study the Bible:
Ezekiel ch.33 v11
John ch.3 v16-17
1 John ch.2 v2

THE WORK OF THE HOLY SPIRIT
His Personal Being and Deity

The Holy Spirit is a person
- It is the unity of the Godhead: Father, Son and Holy Spirit.
- Whom the Father will send in my name and it is a person.
- He will teach you everything and will remind you of everything Jesus has told you.
- Those who are controlled by the Holy Spirit.
- Think about things that please the Spirit.

But the Counsellor, the Holy Spirit, whom the Father will send in my name, will teach you all things and will remind you of everything I have said to you. John ch.14 v26

I would advise you to study the Bible:
Matthew ch.28 v19-20
John ch.15 v26-27
Romans ch.8 v5

Elsewhere we find reference to the following
- Being born again by the Holy Spirit, and
- Living by the Holy Spirit.
- Lying and blasphemy against the Holy Spirit, and
- Not bringing sorrow to God's Holy Spirit by the way you live.

But the fruit of the Holy Spirit is love, joy, peace, patience, kindness, goodness, faithfulness, gentleness, and self-control. Galatians ch.5 v22-23

I would advise you to study the Bible:
Matthew ch.12 v31-32
John ch.3 v5-8
Acts ch.5 v3
Ephesians ch.4 v30

Also, with reference to the Holy Spirit

- The Holy Spirit came on Bezalel of the tribe of Judah with skill, ability and knowledge.
- He came on Samson with power so that he tore the lion apart, and
- The ropes on his hands became like charred flax and the binding dropped from his hands.

I would advise you to study the Bible:
Exodus ch.31 v3-5
Judges ch.14 v5-6; ch.15 v14-15

THE WORK OF THE HOLY SPIRIT
The Divine Executor

In relation to Christ

- I will send the Holy Spirit to you.
- And the Holy Spirit will bring glory to Jesus.
- He is revealed as the Spirit of Christ, and
- He controls each Christian.

If anyone does not have the Spirit of Christ, he does not belong to Christ. Romans ch.8 v9

I would advise you to study the Bible:
John ch.16 v7; ch.16 v14
Romans ch.8 v10
1 Peter ch.1 v11

In relation to the Scriptures
- The Holy Spirit spoke long ago regarding the Scriptures.
- All the Scriptures are inspired by God, and
- He will guide you to the truth.

The Sprit of Truth comes, he will guide you into all the truth. He will not speak on his own; but he will speak only what he hears, and he will tell you what is yet to come. John ch.6 v13

I would advise you to study the Bible:
Acts ch.1 v16-17
2 Timothy ch.3 v16-17

In relation to the world
- When you send your Spirit, they will be created.
- Until the Spirit is poured upon us and then the earth will be magnificent.
- He will convict the world of its sin, and of God's righteousness, and of the coming judgement.

I would advise you to study the Bible:
Psalm ch.104 v30
Isaiah ch.32 v14-15
John ch.16 v8-11

In relation to The Church
- Which God lives as a dwelling by his Holy Spirit.
- The gifts of the Holy Spirit are distributed according to God's will.
- God testified to it by signs and wonders and various miracles.

God also testified to it by signs, wonders and various miracles, and gifts of the Holy Spirit distributed according to his will. Hebrews ch.2 v4

See Ephesians ch.2 v22

In relation to the individual
- We do not know what God wants us to pray for.
- The Sprit intercedes for us in accordance with God's will.
- God has revealed it to us by his Spirit for those who love him.
- The Sprit helps us in our weakness, and
- He pleads for us in our prayers.
- Using the Spirit's words to explain spiritual truths, and
- The Spirit searches even God deep secrets.

I would advise you to study the Bible:
Romans ch.8 v26-27
1 Corinthians ch.2 v9-15

THE WORK OF THE HOLY SPIRIT
God's Approach to the Sinner

God's approach to the sinner
- I was sinful at birth when my mother conceived me.
- I am unspiritual, sold as a slave to sin.
- I do not understand what I do, the evil, this I keep on doing.
- He has freed you from the power of sin that leads to death.

Surely I have been a sinner from birth, sinful from the time when my mother conceived me. Psalm ch.51 v5

See Romans ch.7 v14-20; ch.8 v1-2

Anticipating grace
- The just requirement of the law would be fully satisfied for us.
- But God is so rich in mercy, and he loved us so much.
- That even though we were dead because of our sins.
- God saved you by his grace when you believed.
- Salvation is not a reward for the good things we have done, and
- He has created us anew in Christ Jesus.

It is by grace you have been saved. Ephesians ch.2 v5

I would advise you to study the Bible:
Romans ch.8 v4
Ephesians ch.2 v4, v8-10

The effectual call
- By taking God's word to others.
- Some seed fell on the footpath, only to have Satan comes at once and took it away.
- Some seed fell on rocky ground, but since they don't have deep roots, they don't last long.
- Some seed fell among thorns, but all too quickly so no fruit is produced.

- Some seed fell on good soil, accepted God's Word and produced a harvest.
- God's gift and his call can never be withdrawn.

For God's gifts and his call are irrevocable. Romans ch.11 v29

See Mark ch.4 v13-20

THE WORK OF THE HOLY SPIRIT
Repentance

Repentance
- Do you want evidence that faith without good deeds is useless?
- When the Holy Spirit comes, he will convict the world of guilt.
- Godly sorrow bring repentance that leads to salvation and leaves no regret.
- The Holy Spirit gives birth to spiritual life.

And when he (the Holy Spirit) comes, he will convict the world of guilt in regard to sin and righteousness and judgement. John ch.16 v8

I would advise you to study the Bible:
John ch.3 v6-8
2 Corinthians ch.7 v10
James ch.2 v20

This repentance is often accompanied with a change of plan and action
- Blot out the stain of my sins.
- Wash me clean from my guilt.
- Purify me from my sin.
- Turn from the evil road you are travelling and from the evil things you are doing.
- Perhaps he will forgive your evil thoughts.
- When God changed his mind and did not carry out the destruction he had threatened.
- For no one can ever be made right with God by doing what the law commands.

When God saw what they did and how they turned from their evil ways, he had compassion and did not bring upon them the destruction he had threatened. Jonah ch.3 v10

I would advise you to study the Bible:

Psalm ch.51 v1-2
Jeremiah ch.25 v5
Acts ch.8 v22-23
Romans ch.3 v20

THE WORK OF THE HOLY SPIRIT
Conversion

Conversion
- He saved us, not because of the righteous things we had done, but because of his mercy.
- It is by confessing with your mouth that you are saved.
- If he doesn't obey God's commandments, that person is a liar and is not living in the truth.
- Like newborn babies, you must crave pure spiritual milk.

He saved us, not because of righteous things we had done, but because of his mercy. He saved us through the washing of rebirth and renewal by the Holy Spirit. Titus ch.3 v5

I would advise you to study the Bible:
Romans ch.10 v9-10
1 Peter ch.2 v2-3
1 John ch.2 v4-6

Temporary conversions
- Cling to your faith in Christ, and keep your conscience clear.
- Demas has deserted him because he loves the things of this life.
- When people left, it proved that they did not belong with the churches.
- But since they don't have deep roots, they don't last long, so
- God set another time for entering his rest, and that time is today.

They went out from us, but they did not really belong to us. 1 John ch.2 v19

I would advise you to study the Bible:
Matthew ch.13 v20-21
1 Timothy ch.1 v19-20
2 Timothy ch.4 v10
Hebrews ch.4 v6-7

Repeated conversions

- Look how far you have fallen, turn back to me and do the works you did at first.
- I gave her time to repent but she does not want to turn from her immorality, so
- Be diligent and turn from your indifference.
- Repent of your sin or God will come suddenly to you.

Remember the height from which you have fallen! Repent and do the things you did at first. If you do not repent, I will come to you and remove your lampstand from its place. Revelation ch.2 v5

See Revelation ch.2 v16, v21; ch.3 v3, v19-20

THE WORK OF THE HOLY SPIRIT
Justification and Sanctification

Justification
- God, with undeserved kindness, declares that we are righteous.
- He did this through Christ Jesus.
- When he freed us from the penalty for our sins.
- He will certainly save us from God's condemnation.

Since we have now been justified by his blood, how much more shall we be saved from God's wrath through him! Romans ch.5 v9

See Romans ch.3 v24

Sanctification
- For you have stripped off your old sinful nature and all its wicked deeds.
- Throw off your former way of life.
- Which is corrupted by lust and deception.
- Put on your new nature, created to be like God—truly righteous and holy.
- We are instructed to turn from godless living and sinful pleasures.

It teaches us to say "No" to ungodliness and worldly passions. and to live self-controlled, upright and godly lives in this present age. Titus ch.2 v12

I would advise you to study the Bible:
Ephesians ch.4 v22-24
Colossians ch.3 v9-10

THE WORK OF THE HOLY SPIRIT
The Intermediate State

What will happen to the righteous ones?
- Jesus replied on the cross, "You will be with me in paradise."
- After death, for then we would be at home with the Lord.
- Paul longed to go and be with Christ which would be far better for him.
- You have come to the spirits of the righteous ones in heaven, who
- Have been now made perfect.

Jesus answered him, "I tell you the truth, today you will be with me in paradise." Luke ch.23 v43

I would advise you to study the Bible:
2 Corinthians ch.5 v8
Philippians ch.1 v23-24
Hebrews ch.12 v23

What happens when the righteous are dead?
- To the believers who have died, so you will not grieve like people who have no hope.
- After death, the person is only asleep and Jesus can wake him up.
- Jesus died and he was raised from the dead, and
- He was seen by lots of people; some of them are still alive.
- So we believe that God will bring with Jesus those who died.

I would advise you to study the Bible:
Matthew ch.9 v23-25
1 Corinthians ch.15 v5-8
1 Thessalonians ch.4 v13-14

THE WORK OF THE HOLY SPIRIT
Final Perseverance

Everyone who is saved and not just the few
- God wants all men to be saved and to understand the truth, and
- Not only our sins but the sins of all the world.
- He takes no pleasure in the death of the wicked.
- Everyone who believes in Jesus will not perish but have eternal life.
- For many are called, but few are chosen.

For many are invited, but few are chosen. Matthew ch.22 v14

I would advise you to study the Bible:
Ezekiel ch.33 v11
John ch.3 v16-17
1 Timothy ch.2 v3-4
1 John ch.2 v2

So as believers we might fall away
- They receive it with joy, but they don't last long, and so no fruit is produced, and
- They then turn away from God.
- Then reject the command they were given to live a holy life.
- Do these things, and you will never fall away.
- Christ suffered for you leaving you an example, but
- The one who endures to the end will be saved.
- Eventually, Jesus will come and remove your lampstand from its place among the churches.

But he who stands firm to the end will be saved. Matthew ch.24 v13

I would advise you to study the Bible:
Matthew ch.13 v18-23
Hebrews ch.4 v1; ch.6 v4-6
2 Peter ch.1 v10; ch.2 v21
Revelation ch.2 v5

The eternal security of the Christian

- God chose them and he called them to come to him.
- Nothing in all creation will ever be able to separate us from the love of God.
- The Spirit is God's guarantee that he will give us the inheritance he promised.
- We will continue God's work until it is finally finished on the day when Christ Jesus returns.
- Jesus said, "I give them eternal life and they shall never perish."

No anything else in all creation, will be able to separate us from the love of God. Romans ch.8 v39

I would advise you to study the Bible:
John ch.10 v28-29
Romans ch.8 v30
Ephesians ch.1 v13-14
1 Peter ch.1 v5

THE CHURCH
Purpose and Nature of The Church

The purpose of The Church
- Jesus Christ is head of the church.
- The church was made full and complete, and
- It is to display God's wisdom.

He is the head of the body, the church. Colossians ch.1 v18

See Ephesians ch.1 v22-23; ch.3 v10

The nature of The Church
- The church became stronger as the believers lived in the fear of the Lord.
- These people left our churches because they never really belonged to us, and
- The sufferings of Christ that continue in the church.

It grew in numbers, living in the fear of the Lord. Acts ch.9 v31

I would advise you to study the Bible:
Colossians ch.1 v24
1 John ch.2 v19

The work of The Church
- Christ is head over all things for the benefit of the church and it is his body.
- He has brought you into his own presence, and you are holy and blameless as you stand before him.
- Don't drift away from the assurance you received when you heard the Good News.
- All of you are Christ's body and each of you are part of it.
- Here are some gifts that God has provided and their responsibility to equip God's people.
- But earnestly desire the most helpful gifts, and

- Make every effort to keep yourselves united in the Spirit, binding yourselves together with peace.
- Just as you have been called to one glorious hope for the future.
- To do his work and build up the church, so Jesus is first in everything.

I would advise you to study the Bible:
1 Corinthians ch.12 v27-31
Ephesians ch.1 v22-23; ch.4 v3-6, v11-13
Colossians ch.1 v18-23

THE CHURCH
The Church is Intended to Help

The individual relationship to The Church
- In the church they devote themselves to the teaching, fellowship, sharing in meals and prayer.
- Just as our bodies have parts and each part has a special function to do good.
- The parts we regard as less honourable are those we clothe with the greatest care.
- As each part does its own special work, it helps the other parts grow.
- Says Paul, "I, too, try to please everyone in everything I do."
- Obey your spiritual leaders, and do what they say.
- Are any of you sick? You should call for the elders of the church to come and pray over you.
- Go privately and point out the sins against you, if the other person listens to you and confesses it.
- If the person still refuses to listen take your case to the church.
- Let us not neglect our meeting together, as some people do,

Obey your leaders and submit to their authority. Hebrews ch.13 v17

I would advise you to study the Bible:
Matthew ch.18 v15-17
Acts ch.2 v42
Romans ch.12 v4-5
1 Corinthians ch.10 v30-32; ch.12 v14-26
Ephesians ch.4 v14-16
Hebrews ch.10 v25
James ch.5 v14-15

THE CHURCH
The Ministerial Office

Christ is head over all The Church
- God has put all things under the authority of Christ.
- The body is a unit, though it is made up of many parts.
- Jesus has other believers and not Jews or Gentiles.
- He has taught the apostles and they share his teachings.

I have other sheep that are not in this sheep pen. I must bring them also. John ch.10 v16

I would advise you to study the Bible:
Acts ch.2 v42
1 Corinthians ch.12 v12-13
Ephesians ch.1 v22

The ministerial office
- Our Lord has provided gifts for his church.
- To equip God's people for works of service.
- This is so that the body of Christ may be built up.
- So as to be a holy priesthood.

To prepare God's people for works of service, so that the body of Christ may be built up. Ephesians ch.4 v12

I would advise you to study the Bible:
Ephesians ch.4 v11
1 Peter ch.2 v5

The permanent ministry
- Deacons must be well respected and have integrity.
- They must be committed to the faith, they must be men and have children.
- An elder must be a man whose life is above reproach.
- He must be gentle and not love money and must manage his children well, and

- He must not be a new believer and work hard at preaching and teaching.
- He must have a strong belief and must enjoy having guests.

I would advise you to study the Bible:
1 Timothy ch.3 v1-13; ch.5 v17
Titus ch.1 v6-9
1 Peter ch.5 v2-5

Church daily activities
- The apostles teaching and to the fellowship, to the sharing of meals and to prayer.
- He who eats the bread or drinks the cup of the Lord in an unworthy manner will be guilty of sinning.
- On the first day of the week set aside a sum of money you have earned.
- Don't merely listen to the Word; you must do what it says.

They devoted themselves to the apostles' teaching, and to the fellowship, and to the breaking of bread and to prayer. Acts ch.2 v42

I would advise you to study the Bible:
Acts ch.12 v5
1 Corinthians ch.11 v27; ch.16 v2
James ch.1 v22

THE CHURCH
The Means of Grace

The Holy Spirit
- He is the Holy Spirit who leads you into truth, and you know him.
- Then you will receive the gift of the Spirit.
- But letting the Spirit control your mind leads to life and peace.
- Those who are controlled by the Holy Spirit think about things that please the Spirit.
- The Holy Spirit gives you life because you have been made right with God.

The Sprit of Truth. The world cannot accept him, because it neither sees him, nor known him. John ch.17 v17

I would advise you to study the Bible:
John ch.14 v17
Acts ch.2 v38-39
Romans ch.8 v5-11

Prayer
- Your Father knows exactly what you need even before you ask him.
- The Holy Spirit helps us in our weakness.
- For the Spirit pleads for us believers in harmony with God's own will.
- Don't worry about anything; instead, pray about everything.
- Tell God what you need, and thank him for all he has done.
- We will receive from him whatever we ask because we obey him and do the things that please him.
- The earnest prayer of a righteous person has great power and produces wonderful results.

And we will receive from him anything we ask, because we obey his commands and do what pleases him. 1 John ch.3 v22

I would advise you to study the Bible:
Matthew ch.6 v7-8
Romans ch.8 v26-27

Philippians ch.4 v6-7
James ch.5 v16-17

Bible reading

- Study this Book of the Law continually.
- Meditate on it day and night so you will be sure to obey everything written in it.
- You must remain faithful to the things you have been taught.
- You have been taught the Holy Scriptures from childhood.
- They searched the Scriptures day after day to see if Paul and Silas were teaching the truth.

Do not let this Book of the Law depart from your mouth; meditate on it day and night, so that you may be careful to do everything written in it. Joshua ch.1 v8

I would advise you to study the Bible:
Acts ch.17 v11
2 Timothy ch.3 v14-15

The ministry of the Word of God

- All Scripture is inspired by God and is useful to teach us what is true, and
- It corrects us when we are wrong and teaches us to do what is right.
- Such things were written in the Scriptures long ago to teach us.
- The Scriptures give us hope and encouragement.
- As we wait patiently for God's promises to be fulfilled.
- But one who prophesies strengthens others, encourages them, and comforts them.

But everyone who prophesies speaks to men for their strengthening, encouragement and comfort. 1 Corinthians ch.14 v3

I would advise you to study the Bible:
Romans ch.15 v4
2 Timothy ch.3 v16-17
James ch.1 v21-25

Worship

- Praising God and enjoying all the goodwill of all the people.
- Let the message about Christ, in all its richness, fill your lives.
- Sing psalms and hymns and spiritual songs to God with thankful hearts, and
- Whatever you do or say, do it as a representative of the Lord Jesus.
- Giving thanks through him to God the Father.

Praising God and enjoying the favour of all the people. Acts ch.2 v47

See Colossians ch.3 v16-17

THE CHURCH
Spiritual Gifts

When the Spirit is poured out on all people
- God will pour out his Holy Spirit upon all people.
- God said, "Your sons and daughters will prophesy and your old men will dream dreams.
- Your young men will see visions.
- Even on my servants I will pour out my Spirit in those days."
- "But in the church I would rather speak five understandable words," said Paul.

Afterwards, I will pour out my Spirit on all people. Joel ch.2 v28

I would advise you to study the Bible:
Joel ch.2 v29
Acts ch.2 v17-18
1 Corinthians ch.14 v18-19

A sense that spiritual gifts will make you stronger
- Can bring you some spiritual gift to make you grow strong.
- Do not lack any spiritual gift as you eagerly wait for Jesus to be revealed.
- God will keep you strong to the end.
- So that you will be blameless on the day that Jesus comes again.

You and I may be mutually encouraged by each other's faith. Romans ch.1 v11

See 1 Corinthians ch.1 v7-8

It followed laying on of hands
- When the elders laid their hands on Timothy, and
- He would fan into flames the gift of God.
- For God has not given us a spirit of fear and timidity.

I would advise you to study the Bible:
1 Timothy ch.4 v14
2 Timothy ch.1 v6-7

Each one the manifestation of the Spirit is given for the common good
- Now about spiritual gifts, I do not want you to misunderstand this.
- There are different kinds of gifts, but the same Holy Spirit.
- There are different kinds of service but we serve the same Lord.
- A spiritual gift is given to each of us so we can help each other.
- The Spirit gives them to each one just as he determines.
- Use them well to serve one another.
- If anyone speaks he should do it as one speaking the very words of God.
- If anyone serves he should do it with the strength and energy that God supplies.

About spiritual gifts, brothers, I do not want you to be ignorant. 1 Corinthians ch.12 v1

I would advise you to study the Bible:
1 Corinthians ch.12 v2-11
1 Peter ch.4 v10-11

THE CHURCH
Fasting

In the Old Testament
- Go to the house of the Lord on the day of fasting.
- On the day of fasting you do as you please, and
- Your fasting ends in quarrelling and strife.
- Jehoshaphat resolved to enquire of the Lord and he proclaimed a fast.
- Esther had decreed for them to their times of fasting and mourning.
- Daniel pleaded with God in prayer and fasting.
- They will turn from their evil ways and ask the Lord's forgiveness before it is too late.

So I turned to the Lord God and pleaded with him in prayer and petition, in fasting, and sackcloth and ashes. Daniel ch.9 v3

I would advise you to study the Bible:
2 Chronicles ch.20 v3-4
Esther ch.9 v31
Isaiah ch.58 v4
Jeremiah ch.36 v6-7

In the New Testament
- When you fast do not make it obvious, but
- Only to your Father who sees what you do.
- Jesus said, "When Christ will be taken from them, then the disciples will fast."
- The pharisee fasted twice a week and gave a tenth of all his income.
- While they were worshipping the Lord and fasting, the Holy Spirit spoke to them.
- Paul and Barnabas appointed elders in each church with prayer and fasting.

So that it will not be obvious to men that you are fasting. Matthew ch.6 v18

I would advise you to study the Bible:
Matthew ch.6 v16-17; ch.9 v14-15
Luke ch.18 v12
Acts ch.13 v2; ch.14 v23

THE CHURCH
The Sacraments

Baptism
- Jesus commanded that each person should be baptised.
- The baptism is in the name of the Father and the Son and the Holy Spirit.
- It marks that you must repent of your sins and turn to God.
- The eunuch went down into the water, and Philip baptised him.
- Paul's jailer and everyone in his household were immediately baptised.

At that hour in the night the jailer took them and washed their wounds; then immediately he and all his family were baptised. Acts ch.16 v33

I would advise you to study the Bible:
Matthew ch.28 v19-20
Acts ch.2 v38; ch.8 v36-38; ch.10 v47-48

Holy Communion
- I pass on to you what I received from the Lord himself.
- The bread this is Christ's body which is given for us.
- The wine is the covenant between God and his people.
- It is poured out as a sacrifice to forgive the sins of many people.
- For every time you eat this bread and this cup of wine, and
- You are announcing the Lord's death until he comes again.

For I received from the Lord what I also passed on to you. 1 Corinthians ch.11 v23

I would advise you to study the Bible:
Matthew ch.26 v26-28
1 Corinthians ch.11 v26

THE CHURCH
Tithes and Collections

In the Old Testament God set up the custom of tithing
- Moses said, "You must set aside a tithe of your crops."
- Bring this tithe to the designated place of worship, and
- Eat it there in God's presence.
- The Levites will present an offering from all the tithes to the priests.

You must present a ten of that tithe as the Lord's offering. Numbers ch.18 v26

I would advise you to study the Bible:
Numbers ch.18 v28
Deuteronomy ch.14 v22-23

The Hebrews were expected to offer their tithes
- You may sell the tithe portion of your crops and herds.
- Put the money in a pouch, and go to the place the Lord your God has chosen.
- At the end of every third year, bring the entire tithe and store it in the nearest town.
- Say to the Lord, "I have given it to the Levite, the foreigners, orphans, and widows."

See Deuteronomy ch.14 v25, v28-29; ch.26 v13

In the New Testament it is totally different
- Give your gifts in private, and your Father, who sees everything, will reward you.
- Jesus said this widow has put in more than all the others, she has given everything she has.
- The Philippians gave not only what they could afford, but far more.
- And they did it of their own free will.
- You must each decide in your heart how much to give, and
- They were the only ones who gave Paul financial help.

So that your giving may be in secret. Then your Father, who sees what is done in secret, will reward you. Matthew ch.6 v4

I would advise you to study the Bible:
Matthew ch.6 v3
Luke ch.21 v1-4
2 Corinthians ch.8 v3-5; ch.9 v7-8
Philippians ch.4 v15-16

THE CHURCH
Singing and Music in The Church

In the Old Testament - singing to the Lord
- Listen to the village musicians gathered at the watering holes.
- I heard the voices of men and women singers, and
- They have harps and lyres, tambourines and flutes.
- "But they have no regard for the deeds of the Lord," said Isaiah.

The voice of the singers at the watering places. They recite the righteous acts of the Lord. Judges ch.5 v11

I would advise you to study the Bible:
Ecclesiastes ch.2 v8
Isaiah ch.5 v12

In the Old Testament - when the battle is won or lost
- The Lord had given them cause to rejoice over their enemies.
- Whenever we are faced with any calamity, you will hear us and rescue us, for
- Joy has gone from our hearts, our dancing has turned to mourning.

I would advise you to study the Bible:
Exodus ch.15 v1
2 Chronicles ch.20 v9
Lamentations ch.5 v15

In the New Testament - mourning after a person had died
- Jesus saw the flute players and noisy crowd, and
- He heard the funeral music.

See Matthew ch.9 v23

In the New Testament - a person had survived
- When he came near the house, he heard music and dancing.

See Luke ch.15 v25

In the New Testament - happy to sing
- All of his followers began to shout and sing as they walked along praising God.
- If anyone of you is happy, let him sing songs of praise.
- This great choir sang a wonderful new song.

I would advise you to study the Bible:
Luke ch.19 v37
James ch.5 v13
Revelation ch.14 v3

In the New Testament - in church
- I will sing in the spirit, and I will also sing in words I understand.
- Sing psalms and hymns and spiritual songs to God with thankful hearts.

See 1 Corinthians ch.14 v15

THE CHURCH
Men and Women in The Church

Men only in The Church
- It was not Adam but Eve in the beginning who was deceived.
- Women should learn quietly and submissively.
- They should be silent during the church meetings, and
- It is not proper for them to speak.

I do not permit a woman to teach or to have authority over a man. 1 Timothy ch.2 v12

I would advise you to study the Bible:
Genesis ch.3 v11-12
Acts ch.1 v13-14
1 Corinthians ch.14 v33-35
1 Timothy ch.2 v11-14

Men are called by God
- Jesus only called men to be his disciples.
- Those seven men who are known to be full of the Spirit and wisdom.
- The elders and deacons must be men and each have one wife.

I would advise you to study the Bible:
Mark ch.1 v16-20
Acts ch.6 v3
1 Timothy ch.3 v2; ch.3 v12

Women only in The Church
- Teach the older women to live in a way that honours God.
- Instead, they should teach others what is good.
- These older women must train the younger women to love their husbands and their children.
- To live wisely and be pure, to work in their homes, to do good, and to be submissive to their husbands.
- Each one, brothers and sisters will have spiritual gifts.

Teach the older women to be reverent in the way that they live. Titus ch.2 v3

I would advise you to study the Bible:
Titus ch.2 v4-5
1 Corinthians ch.12 v1-3

THE CHURCH
Homosexuals and Lesbians in The Church

God's wrath against mankind
- God abandoned them to their shameful desires.
- Women turned against the natural way to have sex and instead indulged in sex with each other.
- Men instead of having normal sexual relations with women, burned with lust for each other.
- They suffered within themselves the penalty they deserved.

God gave them over to the sinful desires of their hearts to sexual impurity for the degrading of their bodies with one another. Romans ch.1 v24

See Romans ch.1 v26-27

God's righteous judgement
- All the men from the city said, "Bring them out to us so that we can have sex with them."
- Do not lie with a man as one lies with a woman, it is a detestable sin, and
- You must be cut off from the people.

Do not lie with a man as one lies with a woman; that is detestable. Leviticus ch.18 v22

I would advise you to study the Bible:
Genesis ch.19 v4-5
Leviticus ch.18 v29-30

The acts of sexual immorality
- The acts of the sinful nature are obvious, like sexual immorality.
- Let there be no sexual immorality, impurity, or greed among you.
- Anyone living that sort of life, will not inherit the kingdom of God.
- Having a form of godliness but denying its power, have nothing to do with them.

I would advise you to study the Bible:
Galatians ch.5 v19-21
Ephesians ch.5 v3
2 Timothy ch.3 v1-5

A workman approved by God

- God will change those people's hearts, and they will learn the truth.
- Then they will come to their senses and escape from the devil's trap.
- For they have been held captive by him to do whatever he wants.

See 2 Timothy ch.2 v25-26

THE LAST THINGS
Second Coming of Christ

The second coming of the Lord Jesus
- The Lord himself will come down from heaven.
- He will have a command with the voice of archangel.
- He will have the trumpet call of God.

For the Lord himself will come down from heaven, with a loud command, with the voice of archangel and with the trumpet call of God. 1 Thessalonians ch.4 v16

It will be a single event
- The nations of the earth will see Jesus in the clouds of the sky, with power and great glory.
- There will be deep mourning among all the peoples of the earth.
- Stand and look up, for your salvation is near, for
- There is a great rebellion against God and the man of lawlessness is revealed.

I would advise you to study the Bible:
Matthew ch.24 v30
Luke ch.21 v27-28
2 Thessalonians ch.2 v3

The mode of his coming will be like his ascension
- Jesus will go and prepare a place for you.
- He will come back in the same way as you have seen him go into heaven.
- He said, "I will come back and take you to be with me for ever."

This same Jesus, who has been taken from you into heaven, will come back in the same way you have seen him go into heaven. Acts ch.1 v11

See John ch.14 v3-4

The final purpose of his coming

- The day of the Lord will come like a thief.
- Jesus will come on the clouds of heaven with power and great glory.
- He will be seated in the place of power at God's right hand, and
- He will send out his angels with the mighty blast of a trumpet, and
- They will gather his chosen ones from all over the world.
- But he wanted his own Israelites to become jealous and claim it for themselves.
- Bringing judgement on those who don't know God.
- Then the heavens will pass away with a terrible noise, and
- The very elements themselves will disappear in fire, and the earth and everything on it.

I would advise you to study the Bible:
Matthew ch.24 v30-31
Mark ch.14 v62
Romans ch.11 v11
1 Corinthians ch.15 v23
2 Thessalonians ch.1 v7-8
2 Peter ch.3 v10

THE LAST THINGS
Millennialism

The calling of the Gentiles
- This gospel will be preached in the whole world as a testimony to all nations.
- Until the full number of Gentiles comes to Christ, and
- Then the end will come.

I would advise you to study the Bible:
Matthew ch.24 v14
Romans ch.11 v25-26

The conversion of Israel
- This veil can be removed only by believing in Christ.
- To cleanse Israel for all their sins and impurity.
- Jesus will pour on them a spirit of grace and prayer, and
- Mourn for him as one mourns for an only child.
- For God's gifts and his call can never be withdrawn.

I would advise you to study the Bible:
Zechariah ch.12 v10; ch.13 v1
Romans ch.11 v28-29
2 Corinthians ch.3 v14-15

The great tribulation
- Then you will be arrested, persecuted, and killed.
- "You will be hated all over the world because you are my followers," said Jesus.
- But the one who stands firm to the end will be saved.

Then you will be handed over to be persecuted and put to death, and you will be hated by all nations because of me. Matthew ch.24 v9

See Matthew ch.24 v10-12, v24-25

Signs and wonders
- Immediately after the anguish of those days.
- The sun, the moon, the stars will be darkened and the heavenly bodies will be shaken.
- On earth, nations will be in anguish and perplexity at the sea.
- Men will faint in terror, apprehensive of what is coming on the world.

I would advise you to study the Bible:
Mark ch.13 v24
Luke ch.21 v25-26

The coming of the antichrist
- This is the last hour and you have heard that the antichrist is coming.
- Such a person has the spirit of the antichrist is a deceiver, and
- They deny that Jesus Christ came in a real body.

This is the spirit of the antichrist, which you have heard is coming, and even now is already in the world. 1 John ch.4 v3

I would advise you to study the Bible:
1 John ch.2 v18
2 John ch.1 v7

THE LAST THINGS
Physical Death

Death denotes the separation of the body
- Ahab the king of Israel died and the body was taken to Samaria and buried there.
- With what kind of bodies will they have?
- Then God gives it a new body that he wants it to have, and
- We will have a house in heaven, an eternal body made for us by God himself.

So the king died and was brought to Samaria, and they buried him there. 1 Kings ch.22 v37

I would advise you to study the Bible:
1 Corinthians ch.15 v35-38
2 Corinthians ch.5 v1

Death for the Christian is peaceful
- On the cross Jesus said, "Today you will be with me."
- Paul said, "I long to go and be with Christ, which would be far better for me."
- Do not be surprised at the painful trial you are suffering.
- We know that as long as we live in these bodies, we are not at home with the Lord.

We are confident, I say, and would prefer to be away from the body and at home with the Lord. 2 Corinthians ch.5 v8

I would advise you to study the Bible:
Luke ch.23 v43
Philippians ch.1 v23-24
1 Peter ch.4 v12-13

Death for the great tribulation
- There will be from every nation, tribe, people and language a vast crowd of people.

- These are the ones who died in the great tribulation.
- That is why they stand in front of God's throne and serve him night and day.
- They will never be hungry or thirsty neither will they be scorched by the heat of the sun.
- God will wipe every tear from their eyes.

See Revelation ch.7 v9, v14-17

THE LAST THINGS
After Death, Will I be Asleep and Living?

Sleep of the soul
- Sleep is a relevant symbol for death.
- You will not grieve like persons who have no hope.
- God will bring back the believers who have died.

The girl is not dead but asleep. Matthew ch.9 v24

I would advise you to study the Bible:
Matthew ch.9 v25
Acts ch.7 v60
1 Thessalonians ch.4 v13-14

Life after death
- We will be fully confident and we would rather be away from these earthly bodies.
- After death the righteous will go into paradise and eternal life.
- But the wicked will go into eternal punishment.

They will go away to eternal punishment, but the righteous to eternal life. Matthew ch.25 v46

I would advise you to study the Bible:
Luke ch.16 v22-24
2 Corinthians ch.5 v8

THE LAST THINGS
The Intermediate State

The underworld like Sheol (Old Testament) and Hades (New Testament)
- The wicked will go down to the grave, for
- My life is full of trouble.
- They have left me among the dead.
- God has thrown me into the lowest pit, into the darkest depths, and
- There is neither working nor planning nor knowledge nor wisdom.

The wicked return to the grave, all of the nations that forget God. Psalm ch.9 v17

I would advise you to study the Bible:
Psalm ch.88 v3-7
Ecclesiastes ch.9 v10

After death for the Christian
- The path of life leads upward for the wise.
- They leave the grave behind.
- The poor man will be comforted, but the rich man will be in anguish, and
- No one can cross over, for there is a great chasm between us.

The path of life leads upward for the wise to keep him from going down to the grave. Proverbs ch.15 v24

See Luke ch.16 v25-26

After death the wicked
- But many Israelites will be thrown into outer darkness.
- The rich man said, "I am in anguish in these flames."
- The Lord knows how to rescue godly people from their trials.
- Even while keeping the wicked under punishment until the day of final judgement.

I would advise you to study the Bible:
Matthew ch.8 v12
Luke ch.16 v24
2 Peter ch.2 v9

THE LAST THINGS
Resurrection

The resurrection
- When the Son of Man comes and all the angels with him.
- Jesus will sit on his throne in heavenly glory.
- All those who are in their graves will hear his voice and come out, and
- All the nations will be gathered before him.

All the nations will be gathered before him. Matthew ch.25 v32

I would advise you to study the Bible:
Matthew ch.25 v31-33
John ch.5 v28-29

They will all have new bodies
- God gives it the new body as he has determined.
- We will not all die, but we will all be transformed.
- Those who have died will be raised to live forever.
- He will take our weak mortal bodies, and
- Change them into glorious bodies like his own.

Then God gives it a body as he has determined. 1 Corinthians ch.15 v38

I would advise you to study the Bible:
1 Corinthians ch.15 v51-53
Philippians ch.3 v21

THE LAST THINGS
The Judgement

The dead will be judged
- I saw the dead, both great and small, standing before God's great white throne.
- And the books were opened, including the Book of Life.
- Jesus will judge us for everything we do, including every secret thing.
- Jesus can do nothing on his own, for
- I judge as God tells me.
- The bad angels were waiting for the great day of judgement, and
- Anyone whose name was not found recorded in the Book of Life was thrown into the lake of fire.

God will bring every deed into judgement, including every hidden thing, whether it is good or evil. Ecclesiastes ch.12 v14

I would advise you to study the Bible:
John ch.5 v30
Jude ch.1 v6
Revelation ch.20 v11-15

Everybody will be judged
- For we must all stand before Christ to be judged.
- There will be trouble and calamity for everyone who keeps on doing what is evil.
- For the Jew first and also for the Gentile.
- We will each receive whatever we deserve for the good or evil we have done in this earthly body.
- For God does not show favouritism.

For we must all appear before the judgement seat of Christ, that each one may receive what is due to him for the things done in the body, whether good or bad. 2 Corinthians ch.5 v10

See Romans ch.2 v7-11

The wicked will be separated from the righteous
- Should not the judge of all the earth do what is right?
- Treating the righteous with the wicked alike.
- When you refuse to help the least of your brothers and sisters, and you are refusing to help Jesus.
- They continue to do such evil things and also approve of those who practise them, and
- They will go away into eternal punishment.

Will not the judge of the earth do right? Genesis ch.18 v25

I would advise you to study the Bible:
Matthew ch.25 v41-46
Romans ch.1 v32

THE LAST THINGS
Rewards and Crowns

The rewards
- God will reward you fully for what you have done.
- I give all people their due rewards, according to what their actions deserve.
- For a great reward awaits you in heaven, and
- I am bringing my reward with me to repay all people according to their deeds.

I the Lord search the heart and examine the mind, to reward a man according to his conduct, according to what his deeds deserve. Jeremiah ch.17 v10

I would advise you to study the Bible:
Ruth ch.2 v12
Matthew ch.5 v12
Revelation ch.22 v12

The crowns
- But the crown of righteousness for all who eagerly look forward to the appearing of Jesus.
- God blesses those who patiently endure testing, temptation and death.
- Afterward they will receive the crown of life, and
- You will receive a crown of never-ending glory and honour.

You will receive the crown of glory that will never fade away. 1 Peter ch.5 v4

I would advise you to study the Bible:
2 Timothy ch.4 v8
James ch.1 v12
Revelation ch.2 v10

THE LAST THINGS
The Consummation of all Things

It will be the final purpose
- The Lord is about to destroy the earth and make it a vast wasteland.
- The present heavens and earth have been stored up for fire.
- I am creating new heavens and a new earth, and
- No one will even think about the old ones anymore.
- Then I saw a new heaven and a new earth and there was no longer any sea.

Behold, I will create new heavens and a new earth. The former things will not be remembered, nor will they come to mind. Isaiah ch.65 v17

I would advise you to study the Bible:
Isaiah ch.24 v1; ch.65 v18
2 Peter ch.3 v7
Revelation ch.21 v1

The righteous and the cursed ones
- That future day when God will reveal who his children really are.
- The cursed ones will go away into eternal punishment.
- But the righteous will go into eternal life.
- The animals they will neither harm nor destroy on God's holy mountains.
- The creation looks forward to the day when it will join God's children.
- In glorious freedom from death and decay.

Then they will go away to eternal punishment, but the righteous to eternal life. Matthew ch.25 v46

I would advise you to study the Bible:
Isaiah ch.11 v6-9
Romans ch.8 v19-21

PART 2

We Don't Trust the Bible?

SUMMARY OF 'WE DON'T TRUST THE BIBLE?'

Quite a few readers question the accuracy of the Bible and maintain there are serious issues. But the Old Testament was written in Hebrew and the New Testament was written in Greek. Both were handed down many years ago. Surely, there's some contention that the words have been wrongly written down over the centuries?

Nobody questions the image of God, Jesus Christ and the Holy Spirit, and how they are presented in the Bible. But the important thing to note is that the Bible speaks directly to us. The words are not in one place, they are scattered over all the books of the Bible. The Scripture maintains that God is in control.

God left it to the authors to find a way of saying it, but not as a means of overwriting the pages. He did not ignore the personality and outlook of the person, the person wrote what was true. As true as the people who lived, the outlook, the pressure and the situation looked. If the person lacked the Word of God, they were in a far off country and totally depressed; that was what the writer thought and said.

That why it is important not to miss a section of pages. The whole Bible is sixty-six books long and we are expected to read and study the whole Scripture. That why it is called God's Manual for Living.

So I have collected the areas to show the difference, and you can make your own mind up to see if the Bible is valid. But most important of all is what I have prepared for you under biblical theology. Nobody could doubt that the Bible is true.

WE DON'T TRUST THE BIBLE?
Numbers in the Old Testament

How many fighting men were found in Judah?

- Is the number 500,000 or 470,000?
- Numbers are written as words, and
- It was a very large amount.

Joab reported the number of fighting men to the king: In Israel there were eight hundred thousand able-bodied men who could handle a sword, and in Judah five hundred thousand. 2 Samuel ch.24 v9

Joab reported the number of fighting men to David: In all Israel there were one million one hundred thousand men who could handle a sword, including four hundred and seventy thousand in Judah. But Joab did not include Levi and Benjamin in the numbering because the king's command was repulsive to him. 1 Chronicles ch.21 v4-6

WE DON'T TRUST THE BIBLE?
Misleading Errors

Did Joshua and the Israelites capture Jerusalem?

- The kings of Jerusalem were taken alive and killed.
- But the Jebusites were still living in Jerusalem.
- The king and the Jebusites were very different.

So they brought the five kings out of the cave...the king of Jerusalem. Then Joshua struck and killed the kings and hanged them on five trees. Joshua ch.10 v22-23, v26

Joshua could not dislodge the Jebusites, who were living in Jerusalem; to this day the Jebusites live there with the people of Judah. Joshua ch.15 v63

Did John the Baptist recognise Jesus after his baptism?

- He was in prison but couldn't get out to see, and
- He didn't understand what Jesus was doing.
- He thought, if Jesus was not a king, what was happening?

Then John gave this testimony: "I saw the Spirit come down from heaven as a dove and remain on him. I would not have known him, except that the one who sent me to baptise with water told me, 'The man on whom you see the Spirit come down and remain is he who will baptise with the Holy Spirit.' I have seen and testify that this is the Son of God." John ch.1 v32-34

When John heard in prison what Christ was doing, he sent his disciples to ask him, "Are you the one who was to come, or should we expects someone else." Jesus replied, "Go back and report to John what you hear and see: The blind receive sight, the lame walk, those who have leprosy are cured, the deaf hear, the dead are raised, and the good news is reached to the poor." Matthew ch.11 v2-5

Jesus saw a man sitting at the tax collectors office and called him, what was his name?

- His given name was probably Levi, and
- Matthew was his apostolic name.

As Jesus went on from there, he saw a man named Matthew sitting at the tax collector's booth. "Follow me", he told him, and Matthew got up and followed him. Matthew ch.9 v9

As he walked along, he saw Levi son of Alphaeus sitting at his tax collector's booth. "Follow me," Jesus told him, and Levi got up and followed him. Mark ch.2 v14

WE DON'T TRUST THE BIBLE?
An Observer Witnessed Something Happening

Who killed Saul?

- Saul fell on his spear but wasn't immediately killed.
- He fell on his sword, but was probably alive, and
- The Amalekite slew him.

Saul said to his armour-bearer, "Draw your sword and run me through, or these uncircumcised fellows will come and run me through and abuse me." But his armour-bearer was terrified and would not do it; so Saul took his own sword and fell on it. 1 Samuel ch.31 v4

"I happened to be on Mount Gilboa," the young man said, "and there was Saul leaning on his spear, with the chariots and riders almost upon him. When he turned round and saw me, he called out to me," and I said, 'What can I do?' He asked me, 'Who are you? An Amalekite,' I answered. "Then he said to me, 'Stand over me and kill me! I am in the throes of death, but I'm still alive." So I stood over him and killed him, because I knew that after he had fallen he could not survive. 2 Samuel ch.1 v6-10

Did Manasseh, king of Judah, repent during his last days?

- He humbled himself and repented.
- But the Israelites carried on with the evil practices that he made.
- Because of the wicked things Manasseh son of Hezekiah, did in Jerusalem, and
- God would judge the people.

As for the other events in Manasseh's reign, and all he did, including the sins he committed, are they not written in The book of the annuls of the kings of Judah? 2 Kings ch.21 v17

His prayer and how God was moved by his entreaty, as well as all his sins and unfaithfulness, and the sites where he built high places and set up Asherah poles and idols before he humbled himself - all are written in the records of the seers. 2 Chronicles ch.33 v19

"I will send four kinds of destroyers against them," declares the Lord, "the sword to kill, the dogs to drag away, the birds of the air and the beasts of the earth to devour and destroy. I will make them abhorrent to all the kingdoms of the earth because of what Manasseh son of Hezekiah, king of Judah, did in Jerusalem." Jeremiah ch.15 v3-4

Who was the father or Joseph, husband of Mary?

* Matthew follows the line of Joseph.
* While Luke emphasises that of Mary, the mother of Jesus.

Jacob the father of Joseph, the husband of Mary, of whom was born Jesus, who is called Christ. Thus there were fourteen generations in all from Abraham to David, fourteen from David to the exile to Babylon, and fourteen from the exile to the Christ. Matthew ch.1 v16-17

He was the son, so it was thought, of Joseph, the son of Heli. Luke ch.3 v23

Did Jesus bear his own cross?

* A condemned man would normally carry a beam of it to the execution.
* Along the way Simon probably helped because Jesus was weakened by the flogging.

Finally Pilate handed him over to them to be crucified. So the soldiers took charge of Jesus. Carrying his own cross, he went out the Place of the Skull. John ch.19 v16-17

As they were going out, they met a man from Cyrene, named Simon, and they forced him to carry the cross. Matthew ch.27 v32

WE DON'T TRUST THE BIBLE?
The Arguments of the Religious Leaders

Was John the Baptist, Elijah who was to come?

- John properly denied that he was Elijah.
- But Jesus maintained he was Elijah in what he was doing.

Then his disciples asked him, "Why then do the teachers of the law say Elijah must come first?" Jesus replied, "To be sure, Elijah comes and will restore all things. But I tell you, Elijah has already come, but they didn't recognise him, but have done to him everything they wished." Matthew ch.17 v10-12

This was John's testimony when the Jews of Jerusalem sent priests and Levites to ask him who he was. He did not fail to confess, but confessed freely, "I am not the Christ." They asked him, "Then who are you? Are you Elijah?" He said, "I am not." John ch.1 v19-20

WE DON'T TRUST THE BIBLE?
A Person Might be Forgetful

Apart from Jesus did anyone else ascend to heaven?

- John was thinking about Jesus, and
- He might have forgotten Elijah, who went up to heaven in a whirlwind.

As they were walking along and talking together, suddenly a chariot of fire and horses of fire appeared and separated the two of them, and Elijah went up to heaven in a whirlwind. 2 Kings ch.2 v11

No one has ever gone into heaven except the one who came from heaven - the Son of Man. John ch.3 v13

PART 3

Principles Of Behaviour

PART 6

SUMMARY OF 'PRINCIPLES OF BEHAVIOUR'

The principles of behaviour was written to help you in the time of need. After we have been through and contemplated systematic theology. You can be expected to think, it all right for the others, but what about me? What about the problems I face?

Each one of us will have problems and how we handle the situation will make the difference to our lives before God and our families, looking out for our neighbours and the world. If you tried to get away, and go and live on a desert island, the troubles and worry will still be there.

The reason is that studying the Bible gives a stark reminder of the persons whom the Bible recounts lived their lives, some peaceful, some tragic. We can see our appearance in the words that people wrote down.

I am counted among those who go down to the pit; I am like a man without strength. I am set apart with the dead, like the slain who lie in the grave, who you remember no more, who are cut off from your care. Psalm ch.88 v4-5

One whose life has been lived, so near the trouble has been his years, that he seems to have known that God has abandoned him. Yet even those nearest to him have turned their backs on him. Living on the brink of death, crying out to the Lord for help,

Is that what you are like?

"If you can?" said Jesus. "Everything is possible for him who believes." Immediately the boy's father exclaimed, "I do believe; help me overcome my unbelief!" Mark ch.9 v23-24

A man had a son who was possessed by a spirit that had robbed him of speech. The son foamed at the mouth, gnashed his teeth and became rigid. He said his son had been like this from childhood. The man was crying out for the Lord to help him, and he had seen his boy ruined by the evil spirit. The son couldn't go to school. Most people would avoid his son, and the whole family would be paralysed to help him. But when Jesus met him, Jesus said, "Everything is possible for him who believes." The man cried out, "Help me, I do believe!"

Do you have a child like that?

Why is it a study book?
The principals of behaviour is not complete, I have left you to carry on studying the Bible, with what I am suggesting. Take an example of: 'Abandoned.' If your parents didn't want you close by and they shut the door behind you. Even after all these years, your parents died and didn't forgive you and trust you.

You will have to be calm, placid and not depressed. The Lord will protect and love you and care for you.

There's several other things to bear in mind:
- If you are young and lonely.
- If you have to go into another home.
- What about your relatives?
- What about the ill treatment you have suffered?
- If your parents didn't want you to share with them.
- If you are cut off from your portion of the house.
- Even then you must love your parents.

PRINCIPLES OF BEHAVIOUR
Abandoned

My parents abandoned me
- Even if my parents abandon me, the Lord will hold me close.
- My enemies say nothing but evil about me.
- My best friend, the one I trusted completely has turned against me.
- Jesus said, "You must forgive that person."
- The Lord stood by me so that I might preach the Good News, and
- He rescued me from certain death.

Though my father and mother forsake me, the Lord will receive me. Psalm ch.27 v10

I would advise you to study the Bible:
Psalm ch.41 v5-9
Luke ch.17 v3-4
2 Timothy ch.4 v17-18

PRINCIPLES OF BEHAVIOUR
Afraid

What to do if you are afraid
- I trust God why should I be afraid?
- I praise the Lord for what he has promised.
- When I am afraid I will put my trust in you, what can mere mortals do to me?
- Jesus rebuked the wind and said to the water, "Be still."
- He asked the disciples, "Why are you afraid, do you still have no faith?"

When I am afraid, I will trust in you. Psalm ch.56 v3

I would advise you to study the Bible:
Psalm ch.56 v4, v10-11
Mark ch.4 v35-41

PRINCIPLES OF BEHAVIOUR
Anger

I feel anger and am cross
- A curse on their anger, for it is fierce; a curse on their wrath, for it is cruel.
- For anger gives a foothold to the devil.
- Be free from anger and controversy and control your temper, for anger labels you a fool.
- For a day of anger is coming, when God's righteous judgement will be revealed.

Do not be quickly provoked in your spirit, for anger resides in the lap of fools.
Ecclesiastes ch.7 v9

I would advise you to study the Bible:
Genesis ch.49 v6-7
Romans ch.2 v5-6
Ephesians ch.4 v27

PRINCIPLES OF BEHAVIOUR
Animals

Looking after the animals
- God said, "I made the earth and all its people and every animal."
- Man will reign over the fish, the birds, the livestock and all the animals.
- Against its will, all creation was subjected to God's curse, and
- The Lord will protect all the animals on earth and feed them.

Look at the birds of the air, they do not sow or reap or store away in barns, and yet your heavenly Father feeds them. Matthew ch.6 v26

I would advise you to study the Bible:
Genesis ch.1 v26
Jeremiah ch.27 v4-5
Matthew ch.6 v25
Romans ch.8 v20-21

PRINCIPLES OF BEHAVIOUR
Anxiety

I have anxiety
- So what do people get in this life for all their hard work and anxiety?
- Their days of labour are filled with pain and grief.
- Even at night their minds cannot rest.
- I believed in you, so I said, "I am deeply troubled, Lord."
- In my anxiety I cried out to you, "These people are all liars!"
- What can I offer the Lord for all he has done for me?

What does a man get for all the toil and anxious striving with which he labours under the sun? Ecclesiastes ch.2 v22

I would advise you to study the Bible:
Psalm ch.116 v10-12
Ecclesiastes ch.2 v23

PRINCIPLES OF BEHAVIOUR
Befriend

I have difficulty making friends
- The more productive and useful you will be in your knowledge of our Lord Jesus Christ.
- A friend is always loyal, and a brother is born to help us in time of need.
- God gives wisdom, knowledge and joy to those who please him.
- Those who fail to develop in this way have not been cleared of their old sins.
- Two people can help each other too succeed.

A friend loves at all times. Proverbs ch.17 v17

I would advise you to study the Bible:
Ecclesiastes ch.2 v26; ch.4 v9-12
2 Peter ch.1 v8-9

PRINCIPLES OF BEHAVIOUR
Bereaved

He gives hope to the broken-hearted
- God heals the broken-hearted and bandages their wounds.
- We will not all die, but we will all be transformed.
- He gives us victory over sin and death, and
- God himself will be with them and they shall be his people.
- There will be no more death or sorrow or crying or pain.
- All these things are gone forever.

He heals the broken-hearted and binds up their wounds. Psalm ch.147 v3

I would advise you to study the Bible:
1 Corinthians ch.15 v51-53, v57
Revelation ch.21 v3-4

PRINCIPLES OF BEHAVIOUR
Care

Care for widows
- They people refuse to hear the needy widow.
- They cheat the woman who has no son to help her.
- You must not exploit a widow or an orphan.
- Then God will hear their cry and his anger will blaze against you, and
- Take care of any widow, who has no one else to care for her.

Give proper recognition to those widows who are really in need. 1 Timothy ch.5 v3

I would advise you to study the Bible:
Exodus ch.22 v22-24
Job ch.24 v21

PRINCIPLES OF BEHAVIOUR
Career

Selecting a career
- Give your bodies over to the Lord because of all that he has done for you.
- But let God transform you into a new person by changing the way you think.
- Peoples' loyalty for God and the world are divided, and they are unstable in all that they do.
- You can escape the world's corruption caused by human desires.
- Don't copy the behaviour and customs of this world.
- God has given us great and precious promises.

Do not conform any longer to the pattern of this world. Romans ch.12 v2

I would advise you to study the Bible:
Romans ch.12 v1
James ch.1 v5-8
2 Peter ch.1 v4

PRINCIPLES OF BEHAVIOUR
Death

When the Christian is about to die
- I will not be afraid, for you are walking with me.
- Even when I walk through the darkest valley.
- Jesus will come and get you, so that you will always be with him where he is.
- Don't let your hearts be troubled, trust in God and trust also in Jesus.
- There is no judgement against anyone who believes in Jesus.
- He will have eternal life.
- There will be no more death or sorrow or crying or pain.
- All these things are gone forever.

He will wipe every tear from their eyes. Revelation ch.21 v4

I would advise you to study the Bible:
Psalm ch.23 v4
John ch.3 v16-18; ch.14 v1-3

PRINCIPLES OF BEHAVIOUR
Depression

I feel depressed
- A tormenting spirit from God that filled him with depression and fear.
- Come quickly, Lord, and answer me, for my depression deepens.
- Don't turn away from me, or I will die.
- Let me hear of your unfailing love each morning, for I am trusting you.
- Show me where to walk, for I give myself to you.
- Teach me to do your will, for you are my God.
- May your gracious Spirit lead me forward on a firm footing.

An evil spirit from the Lord tormented him. 1 Samuel ch.16 v14

See Psalm ch.143 v7-10

PRINCIPLES OF BEHAVIOUR
Doubting

Troubled by doubt
- Only fools say there is no God.
- Anything is possible if a person believes.
- Thomas replied, "I will not accept it if I can't see it."
- Jesus replied, "Don't be faithless any longer. Believe!"
- Blessed are those who believe without seeing Jesus.

There is no-one who does good. Psalm ch.53 v1

I would advise you to study the Bible:
Mark ch.9 v23-24
John ch.20 v24-29

PRINCIPLES OF BEHAVIOUR
Drink

Getting drunk
- Night is the time when drinkers get drunk.
- Don't be drunk with wine, because that will ruin your life.
- What ever you drink, do it all for the glory of God.
- Stay alert and be clearheaded.
- Protected by the armour of faith and love.

So whether you eat or drink or whatever you do, do it all for the glory of God.
1 Corinthians ch.10 v31

I would advise you to study the Bible:
Ephesians ch.5 v18
1 Thessalonians ch.5 v6-8

PRINCIPLES OF BEHAVIOUR
Drugs

Getting drugs
- They promise freedom, but they themselves are slaves of sin and corruption.
- I tell you a truth everyone who sins is a slave to sin and whatever controls you.
- They get tangled up and enslaved by sin again, they are worse off, than before.
- They would be better not have known the way to righteousness.
- So if Jesus sets you free, you are truly free.

So if the Son sets you free, you will be free indeed. John ch.8 v36

I would advise you to study the Bible:
John ch.8 v34-35
2 Peter ch.2 v19-20

PRINCIPLES OF BEHAVIOUR
Failure

Troubled by failure
- My health may fail and my spirit grow weak.
- Jesus faced all of the same testing as we do, yet he did not sin.
- Let us hold firmly to what we believe.
- At the throne there we will receive his mercy.
- The Lord will withhold no good thing from those who do what is right.
- We will find grace to help us when we need it most.
- God who is able to keep you from falling away, and
- He will bring you with great joy into his glorious presence.

But God is the strength of my heart. Psalm ch.73 v26

I would advise you to study the Bible:
Psalm ch.84 v11
Hebrews ch.4 v14-16
Jude ch.1 v24

PRINCIPLES OF BEHAVIOUR
Fear

I am frightened by fear
- Do not be afraid of people's scorn, nor fear their insults.
- You will be safe from slander and have no fear when destruction comes.
- You can go to bed without fear, you will lie down and sleep soundly.
- Such love has no fear, because perfect love expels all fear.
- The Lord is my helper, so I will have no fear.
- What can mere people do to me?

The Lord is my helper, I will not be afraid. Hebrews ch.13 v6

I would advise you to study the Bible:
Job ch.5 v20-24
Proverbs ch.3 v24-26
Isaiah ch.51 v7-8
1 John ch.4 v18-19

PRINCIPLES OF BEHAVIOUR
Growing

Not growing spiritually
- Don't judge by appearance or height, but the Lord looks at the heart.
- You have been taught the holy Scriptures from childhood, and
- They have given you the wisdom that comes by trusting in Christ Jesus.
- It corrects us when we are wrong and teaches us to do what is right.
- You are not controlled by your sinful nature, you are controlled by the Spirit of God.
- Why are you trying to become perfect by your own human effort?

The Lord looks at the heart. 1 Samuel ch.16 v7

I would advise you to study the Bible:
Romans ch.8 v9
Galatians ch.3 v3-4
2 Timothy ch.3 v15

PRINCIPLES OF BEHAVIOUR
Guidance

Needing guidance

- Don't copy the behaviour and customs of this world.
- Let God transform you into a new person by changing the way that you think.
- Then you will know God's will for you.
- The Lord will say, "I will guide you along the best pathway from your life," and
- "I will advise you and watch over you."
- But unfailing love surrounds those who trust the Lord.

Then you will be able to test and approve what God's will is his good, pleasing and perfect will. Romans ch.12 v2

See Psalm ch.32 v8-10

PRINCIPLES OF BEHAVIOUR
Happiness

I would be like to be happy

- Give me happiness, O Lord, for I give myself to you.
- How meaningless to think that wealth brings true happiness.
- What sorrow awaits you who are rich, for you have your happiness now, and
- You who are praised by the crowd.
- God's commands, that is where my happiness is found.

Bring joy to your servant, for to you, O Lord, I lift up my soul. Psalm ch.86 v4

I would advise you to study the Bible:
Psalm ch.119 v35-37
Ecclesiastes ch.5 v10-11
Luke ch.6 v24-26

PRINCIPLES OF BEHAVIOUR
Illness

When I am ill
- I am suffering and in pain, rescue me O God.
- For when I am weak, then I am strong.
- I am glad to boast about my weakness, so that the power of Christ can work through me.
- He forgave all my sins and heals all my diseases.
- A prayer offered in faith will heal the sick and the Lord will make you well.
- The earnest prayer of a righteous man has great power and produces wonderful results.

I am in pain and distress; may your salvation, O God, protect me. Psalm ch.69 v29

I would advise you to study the Bible:
Psalm ch.103 v3
2 Corinthians ch.12 v9-10
James ch.5 v14-16

PRINCIPLES OF BEHAVIOUR

Immorality

Sexual immorality
- Not in lustful passions like the pagans who do not know God and his ways.
- When you follow the desires of your sinful nature, the results are very clear.
- Don't fool yourself those who indulge in sexual immorality and other sins like that.
- Nobody living that sort of life will not inherit the kingdom of God.
- Each of you will control his own body and live in holiness and honour.
- But in rejecting God, who gives his Holy Spirit to you.

Do you not know that the wicked will not inherit the kingdom of God. 1 Corinthians ch.6 v9

I would advise you to study the Bible:
1 Corinthians ch.6 v10
Galatians ch.5 v19-21
1 Thessalonians ch.4 v4-8

PRINCIPLES OF BEHAVIOUR
Inadequate

God chose the foolish things
* In the insults, hardships, persecutions and troubles that I suffer for Christ.
* Few of you were wise in the world's eyes, or powerful, or wealthy.
* God chose the foolish things to shame those who are powerful.
* God's grace is sufficient for all your needs, his power works best in weakness, and
* For when I am weak, then I am strong.
* I know how to live on almost nothing.
* I have learned the secret of living in every situation, and
* The Lord will work out the plans for my life.

The Lord will fulfil his purpose for me. Psalm ch.138 v8

I would advise you to study the Bible:
1 Corinthians ch.1 v26-29
2 Corinthians ch.12 v9-10
Philippians ch.4 v12-13

PRINCIPLES OF BEHAVIOUR
Insulted

Troubled by insults
* The insults of those who insult God have fallen on me.
* When I weep and fast they scoff at me.
* When I dress to show sorrow, they make fun of me.
* I am the favourite topic of the town's gossip.
* Jesus did not retaliate when he was insulted nor threaten revenge when he suffered.
* He left his case in the hands of God who always judges fairly.
* The Scripture gives us hope and encouragement as we wait patiently for God.

Instead, he entrusted himself to him who judges justly. 1 Peter ch.2 v23

I would advise you to study the Bible:
Psalm ch.69 v9-12
Romans ch.15 v3-4

PRINCIPLES OF BEHAVIOUR
Jealousy

Troubled by jealousy
- Don't become conceited or provoke one another.
- If there is jealousy and selfish ambition.
- There you will find discord and evil of every kind.
- Not that I was ever in need, for I have learned how to be content with whatever I have.
- I know how to live on almost nothing or with everything.
- I have leaned the secret of living in every situation.

Let us not become conceited, provoking and envying each other. Galatians ch.5 v26

I would advise you to study the Bible:
Philippians ch.4 v11-12
James ch.3 v16

PRINCIPLES OF BEHAVIOUR
Lie

Don't tell lies
- When Satan lies it is consistent with his character.
- He is a liar and the father of lies.
- Stop telling lies and let us tell our neighbours the truth.
- All liars, their fate is in the fiery lake of burning sulphur after the judgement.

Speak truthfully to his neighbour. Ephesians ch.4 v25

I would advise you to study the Bible:
John ch.8 v44
Revelation ch.21 v8

PRINCIPLES OF BEHAVIOUR
Lost

Jesus came to save those who are lost
- You lived in this world without God and without hope.
- Some wandered into the wilderness and were lost and homeless.
- Once you were far away from God.
- But now you have been brought near to him.
- Jesus came to seek and save those who were lost.
- He led them straight to safety, to a city where they could live.

For the Son of Man came to seek and save what was lost. Luke ch.19 v10

I would advise you to study the Bible:
Psalm ch.107 v4-7
Ephesians ch.2 v12-13

PRINCIPLES OF BEHAVIOUR

Love

Needing Christ's love

- Love never gives up, never loses faith.
- Love your enemies!
- Do good to them.
- Lend to them without expecting to be repaid.
- Then your reward from heaven will be very great.
- Jesus will love them and reveal himself to each of them.
- Nothing can ever separate us from God's love that is revealed in Jesus.

It always protects, always trusts, always hopes, always perseveres. 1 Corinthians ch.13 v7

I would advise you to study the Bible:
Luke ch.6 v32-36
John ch.14 v21
Romans ch.8 v39

PRINCIPLES OF BEHAVIOUR
Medicine

Is it all right if I take medicine?
- There is no one to help you or to bind up your injury.
- Is there no physician there?
- Or medicine to heal you?
- In heaven, the leaves of the tree of life were used for medicine to heal the nations.

The leaves of the tree are for the healing of the nations. Revelation ch.22 v2

See Jeremiah ch.8 v21-22; ch.30 v12-13; ch.51 v8-9

PRINCIPLES OF BEHAVIOUR
Peace

Needing peace
- We can rejoice when we run into problems and trials.
- They help us to develop endurance.
- Let everyone see that you are considerate in all you do.
- We have peace with God because of what Jesus Christ has done for us.
- Jesus said, "I am leaving you with a gift, peace of mind and heart."
- The peace I give is a gift the world cannot give.
- So don't be troubled or afraid.
- Tell God what you need, and thank him for all he has done.
- Remember, the Lord is coming soon.

Peace I leave with you; my peace I give you. John ch.14 v27

I would advise you to study the Bible:
John ch.14 v28
Romans ch.5 v1-3
Philippians ch.4 v4-7

PRINCIPLES OF BEHAVIOUR
Persecuted

Troubled by persecution
- We are not crushed.
- We are perplexed but not driven to despair.
- We are hunted down, but never abandoned by God.
- If God is for us, who can be against us?
- Who then will condemn us?
- The victory is ours through Christ Jesus, who loves us.
- Paul was convinced that nothing can separate us from God's love.
- Call on the Lord when you are in trouble and need help.

Call upon me in the day of trouble; I will deliver you, and you will honour me. Psalm ch.50 v15

I would advise you to study the Bible:
Romans ch.8 v31-34, v38-39
2 Corinthians ch.4 v8-9

PRINCIPLES OF BEHAVIOUR
Praying

Needing prayer
- Keep on asking, and you will receive what you ask for.
- We also know that he will give us what we ask for.
- Jesus said, "This is how you should pray."
- If I had not confessed the sin in my heart, and
- The Lord would not have listened.
- We are confident that he hears us, whenever we ask for anything that pleases him.
- The earnest prayer of a righteous person has great power and produces wonderful results.

The prayer of a righteous man is powerful and effective. James ch.5 v16

I would advise you to study the Bible:
Psalm 66 v18-19
Luke ch.11 v2-4, v9-10
1 John ch.5 v14-15

PRINCIPLES OF BEHAVIOUR
Revenge

About possible revenge
- Jesus did not retaliate when he was insulted.
- Jesus did not threaten revenge when he suffered.
- Always try to do good to each other and to all the people.
- Never pay back evil with more evil.
- Said Paul, "Never take revenge."
- Leave that to the righteous anger of God.

Make sure that nobody pays back wrong for wrong, but always try to be kind to each other and to everyone else. 1 Thessalonians ch.5 v15

I would advise you to study the Bible:
Romans ch.12 v17-19
1 Peter ch.2 v24

PRINCIPLES OF BEHAVIOUR
Shame

I am shameful
- For to your shame I say that some of you don't know God at all, and
- I cling to your laws.
- Lord, don't let me be put to shame.
- The wise inherit honour, but fools are put to shame.
- God chose those things in order, to shame those who think they are wise.
- He chose things despised by the world, things counted as nothing at all.

The wise inherit honour, but fools he hold up to shame. Proverbs ch.3 v35

I would advise you to study the Bible:
Psalm ch.119 v30-32
1 Corinthians ch.1 v27-28; ch.15 v34

PRINCIPLES OF BEHAVIOUR
Sinning

I have committed a terrible sin

- They thought it foolish to acknowledge God.
- He abandoned them to their foolish thinking.
- They refuse to understand, break their promises, heartless, and have no mercy.
- But if we confess our sins to him, he is faithful and just.
- To forgive us our sins and to cleanse us from all wickedness.
- Remember the Lord forgave you, so you must forgive others.

Bear with each other and forgive whatever grievances you may have against one another. Forgive as the Lord forgave you. Colossians ch.3 v13

I would advise you to study the Bible:
Romans ch.1 v28-31
1 John ch.1 v8-10

PRINCIPLES OF BEHAVIOUR
Slavery

God would rescue us from slavery
- He chose them and they would grow strong.
- Then with a powerful arm God led them out.
- He has broken the chain of slavery.
- He rescued them from those who enslaved them.
- You must give yourself to be slaves to righteous living, and
- Jesus Christ has truly set us free.

Do not let yourself be burdened by a yoke of slavery. Galatians ch.5 v1

I would advise you to study the Bible:
Ezekiel ch.34 v27-28
Acts ch.13 v17-20
Romans ch.6 v19

PRINCIPLES OF BEHAVIOUR
Stealing

Tempted to steal
- If you are a thief, you must not steal.
- Don't love money, be satisfied with what you have.
- For God has said, "I will never fail you nor abandon you."
- Instead use your hands for good work, and then give generously to others in need.
- Love does no wrong to others.
- So love fulfils the requirements of God's law.

Keep you lives free from the love of money, and be content with what you have.
Hebrews ch.13 v5

I would advise you to study the Bible:
Romans ch.13 v9-10
Ephesians ch.4 v28-29

PRINCIPLES OF BEHAVIOUR
Suffering

Why does God allow suffering?
- God made the world free from suffering.
- It is from man that suffering comes and defiles us.
- All these vile things come from within your heart.
- Eventually God will wipe every tear from our eyes.
- There will be no more death, or sorrow, or crying or pain.
- All these things will be gone forever.

Then God saw all that he had made, and it was very good. Genesis ch.1 v31

I would advise you to study the Bible:
Mark ch.7 v20-23
Revelation ch.21 v4

PRINCIPLES OF BEHAVIOUR
Suicide

My life is full of troubles
- My body and soul are wasting away and I am dying from grief.
- I am ignored as if I were dead, as if I were a broken pot.
- My life is full of troubles and death draws near.
- I am as good as dead, like a strong man with no strength left.
- Don't you realise that you are the temple of God?
- That the Spirit of God lives in you?

For my soul is full of trouble and my life draws near the grave. Psalm ch.88 v3

I would advise you to study the Bible:
Psalm ch.31 v9-12; ch.88 v4
1 Corinthians ch.3 v16-17

PRINCIPLES OF BEHAVIOUR
Teaching

I would like to get more teaching
- The teaching of God's Word, even the simple can understand.
- Jesus said, "Anyone who listen to my teaching and follows it is wise."
- The elder in the church must be able to encourage others with wholesome teaching.

The entrance of your words gives light; it gives understanding to the simple.
Psalm ch.119 v130

I would advise you to study the Bible:
2 Chronicles ch.17 v9
Matthew ch.7 v26-27
Titus ch.1 v9

PRINCIPLES OF BEHAVIOUR
Unemployment

I am unemployed
- Not that I was ever in need.
- For I have learned how to be content with whatever I have.
- I know how to live on almost nothing or with everything.
- Be still in the presence of the Lord and wait patiently for him to act.
- Once I was young and now I am old, yet
- I have never seen the godly abandoned or their children begging for food.
- Don't worry about evil people who prosper.

Be still before the Lord and wait patiently for him; do not fret when men succeed in their ways. Psalm ch.37 v7

I would advise you to study the Bible:
Psalm ch.37 v25
Philippians ch.4 v11-12

PRINCIPLES OF BEHAVIOUR
Victimisation

I am being victimised
- I have done nothing wrong, yet they prepare to attack me.
- Fierce enemies are out there waiting for me.
- So we can say with confidence,
- The Lord is my helper, so I will have no fear.
- What can mere people do to me?
- Think of all the good that has come from your leaders and follow them.
- Soon the wicked will disappear, and
- Through you look for them, they will be gone.
- Do not lose your temper as it only leads to harm.

I have done no wrong, yet they are ready to attack me. Psalm ch.59 v4

I would advise you to study the Bible:
Psalm ch.37 v8-10; ch.59 v3
Hebrews ch.13 v6-7

PRINCIPLES OF BEHAVIOUR
War

Can a Christian fight?
- We are human and don't wage war as humans do.
- We use God's almighty weapons, not worldly weapons.
- You are jealous of what others have.
- So you fight and wage war to take it away from them.
- Yet you don't have what you want, because your motives are all wrong.
- Jesus said, "You will be hated all over the world because you are my followers."

Nation will rise up against nation, and kingdom against kingdom. Matthew ch.24 v7

I would advise you to study the Bible:
Matthew ch.24 v8-9
2 Corinthians ch.10 v3-5
James ch.4 v1-3

PRINCIPLES OF BEHAVIOUR
Weary

I am so weary
- Jesus said, "Come to me, all of you who are weary and carry heavy burdens."
- He said, "Let me teach you, and you will find rest for your souls."
- That is why we never give up, though our bodies are dying.
- So don't look at the troubles we can see now.
- Rather fix your eyes on the things that cannot be seen.
- How kind the Lord is!
- How good he is!
- I was facing death and he saved me.
- What can I offer the Lord for all he has done for me?

Therefore we do not lose heart. 2 Corinthians ch.4 v16

I would advise you to study the Bible:
Psalm ch.116 v6, v12
Matthew ch.11 v28-29
2 Corinthians ch.4 v17-18

PRINCIPLES OF BEHAVIOUR
Worried

I am very worried
- Don't worry about anything, instead pray about everything.
- His peace will guard your hearts and minds as you live in Christ Jesus.
- See the glorious works of the Lord.
- Be still and know that I am God!
- I will be honoured by every nation, honoured throughout the world.
- That is why I tell you not to worry about everyday life, food, drink or clothes to wear.
- Can all your worries add a single moment to your life?
- God will certainly care for you and he is always ready to help you in times of trouble.
- God is our refuge and strength.

Who of you by worrying can add a single hour to his life? Matthew ch.6 v27

I would advise you to study the Bible:
Psalm. ch.46 v1-3, v8-10
Matthew ch.6 v31-34
Philippians ch.4 v6-7